ISLAM
FOR CHILDREN

Ahmad von Denffer

THE ISLAMIC FOUNDATION

MUSLIM CHILDREN'S LIBRARY

General Editors: **M. Manazir Ahsan** and **Anwar Cara**

ISLAM FOR CHILDREN

Author: **Ahmad von Denffer**

Translator: **Hatifah von Denffer**

Illustrator: **Arshad Gamiet**

Published by
THE ISLAMIC FOUNDATION,

Markfield Dawah Centre,
Ratby Lane, Markfield,
Leicester LE67 9SY, UK
Tel: 01530-244944/5, Fax: 01530-244946
Website: www.islamic-foundation.com
E-Mail: publications@islamic-foundation.com

Quran House, P.O. Box 30611, Nairobi, Kenya

P.M.B. 3193, Kano, Nigeria

Distributed by: Kube Publishing

British Library Cataloguing in Publication Data

Denffer, Ahmad von
Islam for children
1. Islam – Juvenile literature
I. Title II. Islam für Kinder. English
297   BP161.2

ISBN 978-0-86037-085-7 (Paperback)

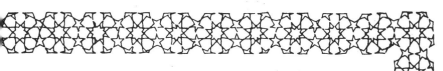

In the Name of Allah
the Merciful, the Mercy-Giving

To Simah, Sulaiman and all other Muslim children

Contents

Foreword

Here is a new series of books, but with a difference, for children of all ages. Published by the Islamic Foundation, the Muslim Children's Library has been produced to provide young people with something they cannot perhaps find anywhere else.

Most of today's children's books aim only to entertain and inform or to teach some necessary skills, but not to develop the inner and moral resources. Entertainment and skills by themselves impart nothing of value to life unless a child is also helped to discover deeper meaning in himself and the world around him. Yet there is no place in them for God, who alone gives meaning to life and the universe, nor for the divine guidance brought by His prophets, following which can alone ensure an integrated development of the total personality.

Such books, in fact, rob young people of access to true knowledge. They give them no unchanging standards of right and wrong, nor any incentives to live by what is right and refrain from what is wrong. The result is that all too often the young enter adult life in a state of social alienation and bewilderment, unable to cope with the seemingly unlimited choices of the world around them. The situation is especially devastating for the Muslim child as he may grow up cut off from his culture and values.

The Muslim Children's Library aspires to remedy this deficiency by showing children the deeper meaning of life and the world around them; by pointing them along paths leading to an integrated development of all aspects of their personality; by helping to give them the capacity to cope with the complexities of their world, both personal and social; by opening vistas into a world extending far beyond this life; and, to a Muslim child especially, by providing a fresh and strong faith, a dynamic commitment, an indelible sense of identity, a throbbing yearning and an urge to struggle, all rooted in Islam.

The books aim to help a child anchor his development on the rock of divine guidance, and to understand himself and relate to

7

himself and others in just and meaningful ways. They relate directly to his soul and intellect, to his emotions and imagination, to his motives and desires, to his anxieties and hopes — indeed, to every aspect of his fragile, but potentially rich personality. At the same time it is recognised that for a book to hold a child's attention, he must enjoy reading it; it should therefore arouse his curiosity and entertain him as well. The style, the language, the illustrations and the production of the books are all geared to this goal. They provide moral education, but not through sermons or ethical abstractions.

Although these books are based entirely on Islamic teachings and the vast Muslim heritage, they should be of equal interest and value to all children, whatever their country or creed; for Islam is a universal religion, the natural path.

Adults, too, may find much of use in them. In particular, Muslim parents and teachers will find that they provide what they have for so long been so badly needing. The books will include texts on the Qur'an, the Sunnah and other basic sources and teachings of Islam, as well as history, stories and anecdotes for supplementary reading. Each book will cater for a particular age group, classified into five: pre-school, 5-8 years, 8-11, 11-14 and 14-17.

We invite parents and teachers to use these books in homes and classrooms, at breakfast table and bedside and encourage children to derive maximum benefit from them. At the same time their greatly valued observations and suggestions are highly welcome.

To the young reader we say: you hold in your hands books which may be entirely different from those you have been reading till now, but we sincerely hope you will enjoy them; try, through these books, to understand youself, your life, your experiences and the universe around you. They will open before your eyes new paths and models in life that you will be curious to explore and find exciting and rewarding to follow. May God be with you forever.

And may He bless with His mercy and acceptance our humble contribution to the urgent and gigantic task of producing books for a new generation of people, a task which we have undertaken in all humility and hope.

M. Manazir Ahsan
Director General

8

PART I

IMAN

بِسْمِ اللهِ الرَّحْمٰنِ الرَّحِيمِ

الْحَمْدُ لِلّٰهِ رَبِّ الْعَالَمِينَ ۝١ الرَّحْمٰنِ الرَّحِيمِ ۝٢

مَالِكِ يَوْمِ الدِّينِ ۝٣ إِيَّاكَ نَعْبُدُ وَإِيَّاكَ نَسْتَعِينُ ۝٤

اهْدِنَا الصِّرَاطَ الْمُسْتَقِيمَ ۝٥ صِرَاطَ الَّذِينَ

أَنْعَمْتَ عَلَيْهِمْ ۝٦ غَيْرِ الْمَغْضُوبِ عَلَيْهِمْ

وَلَا الضَّالِّينَ ۝٧

AL-FATIHA

Bismi-llahi-r-rahmani-r-rahim
Al-hamdu lillahi rabbi-l-alamin
Ar-rahmani-r-rahim
Maliki yaumi-d-din
Iyyaka na'budu wa iyyaka nasta'in
Ihdina-s-sirata-l-mustaqim
Sirata-ladhina an'amta 'alaihim
Ghairi-l-maghdubi 'alaihim wa la-d-dalin

AL-FATIHA

In the Name of Allah, the Merciful, the Mercy-giving.
Praise be to Allah, Lord of the Worlds
The Merciful, the Mercy-giving
Master of the Day of Judgement.
You alone we worship, and You alone we ask for help.
Guide us along the straight path,
the path of those whom you have favoured
not those who earn your anger nor those who go astray.

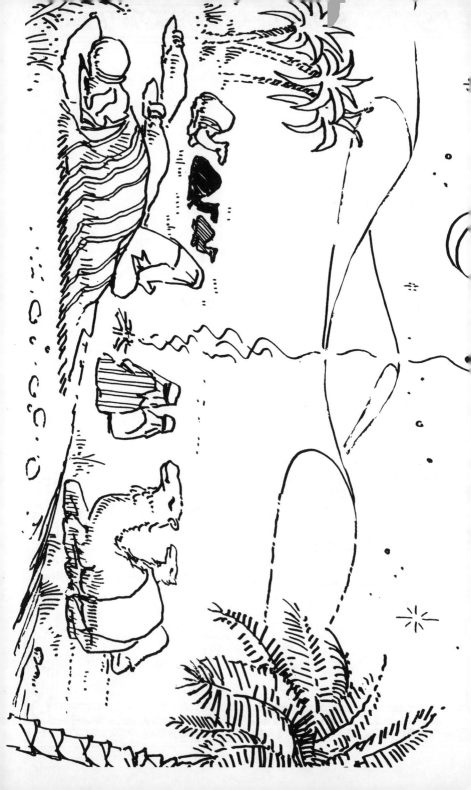

1. Muhammad
(peace and blessings be upon him)

Muhammad was an orphan. His father had died before Muhammad was born and his mother died while he was still very young. This was why Muhammad was brought-up first by his grandfather, Abdul Mutallib, and later by his uncle, Abu Talib. Both of them loved the orphaned Muhammad very much, and both devoted a lot of care to him. When he was big and strong enough to work, Muhammad tended sheep on the outskirts of Makka, the town where he lived.

Muhammad was still a boy when he worked as a shepherd. Later, when he grew into a young man, Muhammad's uncle, Abu Talib, used to take him along on his trading journeys. Makkans like Abu Talib were merchants and the journeys they made were very long. Their camels brought many different goods into Makka. This was a very good and exciting experience for Muhammad and when he grew older he was able to lead the caravans on his own.

In Makka there lived a wealthy widow whose name was Khadija. She owned trade caravans and employed Muhammad to lead them for her. Khadija had made a very wise choice, for Muhammad was a good honest tradesman and a very successful one. Later on, Muhammad and Khadija were married and settled down with their children to lead a happy and peaceful life in Makka.

As the years passed and Muhammad grew older, he began to think deeply about many things.

Although his own family life was very happy, several problems worried him. Muhammad often wandered by the mountains outside Makka and here, in a cave in Mount Hira, he used to sit and think in peace and solitude: I wonder how it happened that I, who was once an orphan, am now such a rich man, Muhammad thought, I have a good wife and loving children, and yet I am still not entirely happy.

Muhammad knew very well why this was so, for he had long been troubled by the situation that existed in Makka: They don't help the poor. They do not bother about caring for orphans or nursing the sick back to health. People in Makka seem to be interested only in having a lot of money and when they have that, they want even more! These thoughts troubled Muhammad for many years.

Then one day, when he was forty years old, Muhammad was in the cave on Mount Hira, and an Angel appeared before him. The Angel, whose name was Gabriel, said to Muhammad: ''Read in the name of your Lord who has created everything, who has created man from a clot of blood.''

At once, Muhammad knew what this meant. He should go to Makka and tell the people: Allah has created Man. Allah has created all the things that Man needs to live. Therefore Man should be grateful to Allah. He should pray only unto Allah and obey only Him. It is Allah's will that the poor and the sick should be cared for, and that people should strive with all their might to do good and lead honourable lives. After death, such people will be richly rewarded for their efforts. But those who purposely do evil will receive terrible punishment, unless they are sincerely sorry for what they have done and ask Allah to forgive them.

At first, Muhammad was very disturbed, for he

had never seen an Angel before. But even so, he realized that the Angel had given him answers to the many questions which had been troubling him. For some time Muhammad had been wondering who it was who had been helping him; now he knew: it was Allah. He wondered why the people of Makka were greedy and mean to the poor; now he knew why: it was because they disobeyed Allah. Allah created Man and all that is in this world, so Man must be obedient to Allah alone.

When Muhammad returned to the city, he told his wife Khadija all that had happened, and all the Angel Gabriel had said. ''Allah will never disgrace you,'' Khadija told her husband, ''for you do many good things. You keep families together. You bear the burden of the weak, you assist the poor and the needy, you entertain the guests and endure hardships in the path of truthfulness.''

Muhammad was very happy that his wife, like himself, believed and trusted in Allah. He began telling his friends of the Angel Gabriel, and what the Angel had said to him. At first, though, only a few people paid attention to what Muhammad said. Most of them just ignored him, for they were far too busy making money, and had no time or inclination to think about Allah.

During this time, and afterwards, the Angel Gabriel continued to appear before Muhammad and always reminded him of the same thing. Muhammad had been chosen as Allah's Prophet, and it was his task to go and tell the people to do good and to worship no other god but Allah. Muhammad must also tell them to spend their money on helping poor people who had too little money themselves.

At last, Muhammad began approaching the people of Makka. He chose beautiful words to tell them of

16

Allah's wishes, hoping that by this means, he would appeal to them: When you have enough to eat and there is a poor man who is hungry, then you must give him some of your food to eat and some of your clothing to wear. The sick must be nursed and the orphans must be cared for. If you do all these things, as Allah wishes, you will be rewarded. But if you refuse, Muhammad warned, you will be punished very severely.

Unfortunately, most Makkans just laughed at what Muhammad told them. Worse still, they refused to worship Allah and went on believing that it was more important to have a lot of money. Some of them even threw stones at the Prophet, and they killed some of those who followed him and believed in Allah alone. Their enmity grew and eventually the people of Makka decided that Muhammad, his family, his relatives and his friends, should be driven out of the town. So they sent them to a valley in the mountains outside of Makka, and nobody was allowed to visit them there or to bring them food. They had to stay in that desolate place for almost three years, and grew so hungry that often they ate the leaves of trees, since they did not have enough food.

Life there was so bad that before long, Khadija, the Prophet's wife, died. Muhammad was very sad. Then the Angel Gabriel appeared and explained to Muhammad that Allah wanted to help him. He should take his friends and family away from Makka and take them to another town, called Madina. The people there were willing to listen to Allah's words, the Angel told Muhammad.

So, Muhammad told his children and his friends to leave Makka and go to Madina. Then all who believed in Allah and worshipped only Allah, left

Makka. The last to leave were Muhammad and his close companion, Abu Bakr. However, the people of Makka were not content with driving Muhammad out. Now they wanted to kill him, because he had been warning them of their evil deeds. But Muhammad was able to leave while the Makkans were on their way to kill him. Ali, Muhammad's brave young cousin, laid himself on Muhammad's bed so that the Makkans would think that the Prophet was still there. But Muhammad and Abu Bakr were long since gone on their way, and so that nobody could find them, they hid themselves in a cave.

When the people discovered that it was Ali who was in Muhammad's bed and that the Prophet had gone, they became very angry. But there was nothing they could do, for Muhammad was already well beyond their evil reach.

Madina was completely different from Makka. Here, Muhammad had more friends than enemies. However, the people of Makka did not leave him in peace. Instead, they followed him to Madina, to make war with him. But Allah helped the Prophet and his followers, and kept them safe from their enemies.

In Madina, Muhammad continued to receive Allah's messages from the Angel Gabriel. These messages were written down in a book, called the Qur'an. In the Qur'an, we can read everything that Allah has said to Man.

The Prophet and his friends built a mosque in Madina and here they prayed five times every day. Once every year, they observed a month of fasting. During the days of this month, they did not eat or drink anything during the daytime. They trained themselves to go without food and drink, for the sake of Allah. From this experience, they learned to get used to eating very little food. So, they had a lot of food left over to give to the poor. They also gave the poor some of their money. Muhammad and his friends believed in Allah and worshipped Him alone. They were obedient to Allah and followed His commands. Therefore they are called Muslims. Those who believe in Allah, who worship Allah alone, and who do things according to the Qur'an, are Muslims.

But those who do not believe in Allah and refuse to obey Him, and even want to kill the Muslims by fighting wars against them, are not Muslims. They are the disbelievers.

For many years, in Madina, Muhammad and his followers had to defend themselves against the attacks of their enemies, and many times were forced to fight against them. But in these battles, Allah gave help to Muhammad and the Muslims. After some time, the disbelievers began to understand that because of Allah's help Muhammad was much stronger than they were. So, at last, they said to themselves: We must stop fighting, for nobody is stronger than Allah. We cannot defeat Muhammad, because Allah helps him. It is therefore better for us also to believe in Allah and to worship Him.

Muhammad and the Muslims were very happy that the long war had at last come to an end. Allah helped them as He had promised, and they were able to return to Makka where they had once been the first small group of people who believed in Allah. When they arrived in Makka, they held a prayer together. After that, some of them remained in Makka, but others who had set up home in Madina went back there. Nevertheless, these Muslims in Madina

journeyed to Makka once a year, because the Ka'ba was there. The Ka'ba is a big stone house with no windows. It looks like a big cube. It was built by Prophet Ibrahim, who lived many years before Muhammad. Whenever you see the Ka'ba, you will be reminded of what Allah has told Mankind, and of what Mankind should do: they should BELIEVE IN ALLAH, WORSHIP ALLAH ALONE AND ALWAYS STRIVE TO DO GOOD. These are Allah's commands to Mankind. Allah has sent many prophets to Mankind, with messages from Him, Who is the creator of Man and the universe. Muhammad was the last of Allah's many prophets, and after he died, he left behind the Qur'an in which all Allah's messages are written down.

In the Qur'an are also many stories of other prophets, who lived long before Muhammad. You will find some of them in this book.

22

2. Allah and the Qur'an

All of Allah's words, which the Angel Gabriel brought to the Prophet Muhammad, are written down in a book. This book is called the Qur'an. In the Qur'an, we can read all that Allah says to us and to all mankind.

In the Qur'an, we can find stories of many other prophets, for Allah always sent prophets to mankind so that they would worship Him alone and do good. That is why there were many prophets before Muhammad.

We can also find many other things in the Qur'an. All that we as Muslims believe, and should do, is written there. When we know what is written in the Qur'an and follow it, we become good Muslims.

All that we know about Allah is what He Himself has told us. Allah told the Angel Gabriel to speak to Muhammad, and Muhammad told the people what the Angel Gabriel had said to him.

Allah is the only God. There is no god apart from Allah. That means, only Allah could have made mankind and the earth, moon, sun and stars. Allah is the only One who created all these.

Of course, you know that many things on earth must work by themselves. For example, when you put seeds in the earth and wait a few months, plants will grow out of them. To put the seeds in the earth is easy, but there is an important question you must ask yourself: Where do we get the earth and from where do we take the seeds? You may say that the

23

eeds can be taken from other plants, and you would e right. But just think: those other plants also need arth to grow in, so where does the earth come rom?

Earth is made out of fine particles of sand, minerals, salts and other materials. Where can we btain the sand and other things from? Plants also eed water to grow, so where does it come from? he plants need sunshine in order to shoot out from he ground. Where do we get sunshine from? We lso need the day and night so that we can count ow many days it takes for the plants to grow.

As we have already said, it is easy to put the seeds the earth and wait till the plants grow out of it, but obody can make all the things that are needed to make it work. No man can make earth and air, light nd water, or the day and the night. It is exactly the ame with all other things.

For instance, man can build houses. He needs tones to do this, but he cannot make the stones imself. Man can also build cars and aeroplanes. To o this he also needs, among other things, iron and ubber. Again, he cannot make iron and rubber mself. Iron can be found in some rocks, and when hese rocks are made hot, the iron turns to fluid and ows out of them. Rubber can be found in certain ees. When the bark of these trees is cut, liquid ubber juice flows out. But the rocks in which the on is found and the trees from which rubber flows ere not made by man. Despite all his cleverness nd skill, man is not able to do these things. This eans that when man makes cars or aeroplanes or anufactures anything else, he is using materials hich are already there on earth. Had they not been ere ready to be used, man could not have made ose cars, aeroplanes and other things. Everything

man uses to make something has been created by Allah. Allah has made all these things which man needs so that people are able to live, build houses, plant crops and rear animals for food and clothing and even make cars and aeroplanes. Without Allah, man would not be able to do anything, for the simple reason that but for the will of Allah, man would not exist. It is Allah Who has created the earth, air, sun, water and the many other things which man needs in order to live. Without these, man cannot live and that means man could not exist on earth. It is Allah Who created man and He Who keeps him alive. Everything is from Allah. That is why we say: There is no god apart from Allah.

It is Allah Who has created everything. Allah has also told man what he should do, because that is good for him. Allah sent prophets to speak to man. Man should always think of Allah and be grateful to Him, and obey the commands He has given through His prophets.

3. Angels

Angel Gabriel brought Allah's words to the Prophet Muhammad and therefore we call Gabriel the Messenger Angel. There are many other angels and we can read about them in the Qur'an.

Each of us has two angels who accompany him. These angels take note of everything we do. They write down our good deeds and our bad deeds. We call these angels the Writing Angels. There are other angels, too. For example, there is an angel who helps people when they die. This angel brings death, so we call him the Angel of Death.

We cannot see the angels because they are made of things which our eyes cannot see. But all the same, we know that they are there, because Allah has told us so. Sometimes, we can even feel the presence of these angels.

Angels are created by Allah, just as man and everything else has been created by Him. Angels obey Allah and are His servants. They perform many tasks and keep the world in being by obeying Allah's commands.

We know that when the sun rises and sets, when the clouds move in the sky, when the raindrops fall, when the plants grow and many other things happen in nature, it is Allah Who has created them and Allah Who sustains them. Nothing can happen without Allah's will. In the same way, Allah created the angels who obey Him. They carry out His will, and take great care that everything goes according to

Allah's will. They are the obedient servants of Allah.

Allah wanted man to obey Him, to pray to Him and to do good. He wanted man to know about Allah. That is why the Angel Gabriel was sent by Allah. The Angel Gabriel told Muhammad what Allah wanted man to do. This was Gabriel's task. Through the Angel Gabriel, Allah had spoken to many prophets before Muhammad, so that man would remember and not forget what Allah wants him to do. We can read about this in the Qur'an. Here there are the stories of Adam, Nuh, Ibrahim, Musa and many other prophets. All of them have said to man:

IN ALLAH ALONE YOU SHOULD BELIEVE
ALLAH ALONE YOU SHOULD WORSHIP
ONLY GOOD DEEDS YOU SHOULD DO

THE HOLY QUR'AN

4. Prophet Adam

Adam was the first man created by Allah. He was created to live on earth. However, Iblis did not like this. Although Iblis was made of fire, he lived with the angels. He thought he was better than Adam, so he became Adam's enemy and decided to make Adam disobey Allah.

Adam and his wife used to live in paradise, where they were put by Allah. Paradise was the most beautiful place you can imagine. It was neither hot nor cold. Adam and his wife were never hungry or thirsty. This was another thing which Iblis did not like. So Iblis came to Adam and his wife and told them to eat from a certain tree. Now, Adam and his wife knew very well that Allah had told them they must not even go near that tree. So they did not listen to Iblis, but Iblis kept on and on at them. He tempted them by saying that they could live for ever if they ate from that tree and would become like angels.

At last, worn down by the nagging of Iblis, Adam and his wife gave in. They came to believe what Iblis was telling them, and they ate from the tree, against Allah's command. But they soon came to regret very much their disobedience and their weakness in listening to Iblis. Adam and his wife were very sad and asked Allah for His forgiveness. Allah forgave them, for He is very forgiving. Allah then told Adam and his wife that they must now go down to earth and live there for some time. But He promised that they would be allowed to return to paradise as lo as they and their children were obedient to Him future.

Allah also told Adam that he would be Allah's fir prophet. Many prophets would be sent to mankin and if man listens to the prophets' words, he w come into paradise when he dies. But if he does n listen, then he will go to hell and remain there wi the evil Iblis.

So, Adam and his wife came down to earth. C earth, they raised their children, and their children their turn raised their children. In this wa succeeding generations of mankind lived on ear and Allah sent His prophets to all of them. The prophets said: Worship only Allah. Allah has creat you. Allah has made for you the plants and t animals so that you can eat them. Be grateful Allah and always do good.

This is what Adam, the first prophet of Allah, to his children. After him there came many oth prophets, and Muhammad is the last of the prophet

بِسْمِ اللهِ الرَّحْمٰنِ الرَّحِيمِ

قُلْ هُوَ اللهُ أَحَدٌ ۝١

اللهُ الصَّمَدُ ۝٢

لَمْ يَلِدْ وَلَمْ يُولَدْ ۝٣

وَلَمْ يَكُنْ لَهُ كُفُوًا أَحَدٌ ۝٤

AL-IKHLAS

Bismi-llahi-r-rahmani-r-rahim
Qul huwa llahu ahad
Allahu samad
Lam yalid wa lam yulad wa lam yaku-lahu
kufuwan ahad

AL-IKHLAS

In the Name of Allah, the Merciful, the Mercy-
giving.
Say: He is Allah, the One
Allah, on whom all ever depend
He does not beget nor was he begotten
And none is like Him.

5. Prophet Nuh
(Noah)

Nuh was a prophet who lived many years after Adam. The people with whom Nuh lived refused to listen to him. When he said that they should worship only Allah and do good, they paid no attention. Nuh told them they would be severely punished for ignoring him and the message he brought from Allah. Even so, the people did not believe what Nuh told them. They laughed at him and said, ''You are only a man like us. Only poor, weak people believe you. If you are telling the truth, then show us the punishment you threaten. You are nothing but a liar!''

''I do not want anything from you,'' Nuh answered, ''and I shall never send away the poor or the weak. As far as the punishment is concerned, Allah will bring it upon you whenever He pleases. Don't imagine you can stop Allah's plans!''

Nuh was both sad and angry that people would not heed his message. But Allah informed Nuh that he should not feel this way. There was much more important work to do. Nuh must build a big ship.

In obedience to Allah's instructions, Nuh began to build the ship on land. The people who saw it when they were passing made fun of him and his ship. But Nuh had a warning for them. ''You are making fun of us now,'' he said, ''but soon we will know who has to suffer the severe punishment!''

When the ship was completed, it started to rain without ceasing and the waters on earth began to

rise. Allah told Nuh to go into the ship, together with his family and all his friends who believed. Nuh should also take one male and one female from each kind of animal on earth.

Nuh did as he was told and then he said, "In the name of Allah, we shall now sail away, and when the time is right, we shall return again to the land."

The waters rose higher and higher until all the valleys were flooded. Nuh saw one of his sons who had not yet boarded the ship and anxiously called out to him, "O my son, climb on board with us so that you will not belong to the unbelievers." But his son refused. Instead, he told Nuh: "I shall go up to the high mountain. The water cannot reach me there."

Nuh became even more anxious. "Only those who listen to Allah can find protection!" he cried out to his son. But just then a huge wave came and many people were drowned. Nuh's son was among them.

It continued to rain for a long, long time. The water rose so high that it covered all the mountains. But at last the rain stopped falling and the floods went down. Now, Nuh's ship landed safely at the side of a mountain and all the people and animals who had been on the ship came out. Nuh and his family and his friends thanked Allah with all their hearts, because they had been saved by Him.

6. Prophet Hud

Many years ago, there lived a very industrious, hardworking people. They were the people of Ad, and they built large and beautiful houses. On every mountain, they had erected a tower and they were very proud of their beautiful buildings.

Among the people of Ad lived a man called Hud, and Hud had been chosen by Allah as His prophet. Allah has sent me to you, Hud said to his people. Allah has taught you all that you are able to do. He has also given you children and many animals. Therefore you should stop worshipping your false gods. Worship only Allah and obey His commands. Do good and do not commit wrongs and evil. Listen to what I say, for if you do not, I fear that a punishment will come upon you.

But the people of Ad scorned Hud: We are not going to listen to you, they scoffed. We are not going to let our gods down, just because you tell us to. Who are you, anyway? You are nothing but a liar. If you are not a liar, then prove it: tell Allah to send us the punishment.

Hud was very sad and disappointed when he heard this. I am not a liar, I am the Prophet of Allah, he said. Do you think the houses you have built will last for ever? Remember that it is Allah Who has given you your fortunes. He is my Lord and your Lord and only in Him do I trust. I have already warned you before: If you don't obey Allah, He will choose some other people to take your place. Allah knows and hears

everything. But despite Hud's warnings, the people of Ad went on worshipping their false gods. Hud was very disappointed. He called his true companions together and with them, he left the people of Ad. In this way, as you shall soon see, Allah protected and preserved those who believed in Him.

Shortly afterwards, a huge black cloud appeared in the sky over the people of Ad. When the unbelievers of Ad saw it, they said: This cloud is surely going to bring us some refreshing rain.

But they were very much mistaken. The cloud brought a terrible wind which killed them all. The wind swept everything away. Nothing was left except a few large stones, which were the remains of the houses and towers. Therefore, it is of no use to build and make many things. If one does not obey Allah, the punishment is sure to come, and all one has built will become ruins.

7. Prophet Salih

The people of Thamud where the Prophet Salih lived
had beautiful gardens. Here there were springs, date
palms and trees which had plenty of fruit. The
houses of Thamud were carved into rocks and
mountains.

Worship only Allah, Salih told his people. You have
no other god apart from Allah, so you should do
good. I am giving you good advice: You should
believe what I say, for Allah has made me His
Prophet.

But only those people of Thamud who were not
rich and not strong believed, and did as Prophet Salih
had said. The rich and powerful people of Thamud
said to Salih: We don't believe what you say and we
are not going to do as you advise. You are nothing
but a man, just like any of us. If you are speaking the
truth, then show us a sign.

Salih brought a camel and said: This camel will be
a sign for you from Allah. Let her graze on Allah's
meadow and let her drink when she is thirsty. Think
of how good Allah has been to you and all that He
has given to you. You should not do evil and cause
trouble on this earth. If you do, a harsh punishment
will fall upon you.

Despite Salih's instructions and teaching, the
proud and powerful people of Thamud still refused to
listen to him. Instead of leaving the camel in peace to
graze in the meadow, they did a very cruel thing:
They cut the tendons on her legs. Thus they openly

broke Allah's command.

Afterwards, they called Salih and said: Now bring us the punishment of which you have been warning us, or we shall not believe that you are the Prophet of Allah.

Salih's promise of disaster came true. After three days, there was a terrible earthquake and all the evil-doers perished. Such was their punishment because they did not obey Allah.

8. Prophet Ibrahim
(Abraham)

Ibrahim was a great prophet. When he was young, he lived among people who refused to worship Allah. Instead they prayed to other things, among them idols which they had made themselves. Once Ibrahim said to his father, "Do you take these idols for gods? If you do, then you and your people are wrong."

Ibrahim knew it was not right to worship idols, for it was against the will of Allah. Allah had also taught Ibrahim many other things. One evening, for instance, Ibrahim saw a bright star in the sky and he said, "That is my God!" But as the star faded away, it became clear to Ibrahim that the star was not God.

On another occasion, Ibrahim saw the moon shining brightly in the night sky, and he again said, "That is my God!" But as the moon disappeared, Ibrahim realized that the moon was not God.

Finally, he saw the bright sun rising at dawn and he said, "That must be my God because it is the biggest thing in the sky." But when sunset came, Ibrahim realized, once more, that this was not God. Only Allah was God. Ibrahim then said, "O my people, I am free from your guilt of worshipping other gods apart from Allah. I firmly and truly turn my face to Him Who created the heavens and the earth, and I shall never worship any god but Allah." Now, Ibrahim wanted to worship Allah alone; He Who is the creator of all these things. For Allah had created the stars, the sun and the moon. Allah is the

Master of the worlds.

Ibrahim went among the people and told them they must worship Allah only. For it is Allah Who created the stars, the sun, and the moon. Allah also created the plants, and animals for food. The sun, moon and stars cannot give anything to eat. Allah has made the earth so that people can live on it. Therefore people should turn away from their false gods and worship Allah alone, and always do good.

Ibrahim spoke of all these things and also said to his father and his people: "What are these images to which you are so devoted?" "Our fathers worshipped them," they replied. "You and your fathers, you have clearly been wrong," Ibrahim rejoined. Then he informed them that they should worship only Allah, who has created everything.

Ibrahim also had a plan for dealing with the idols. When the people were out of the way, Ibrahim broke all their idols and images to pieces. But he left intact and unbroken the biggest idol of all. When the people discovered their idols all smashed and in pieces, they were very angry. "Who has done this to our gods?" they cried. Then some of them remembered that they had heard Ibrahim speaking against their idols. So, they brought Ibrahim and asked him, "Are you the one who did this to our gods, O Ibrahim?" He replied, "No, it was the biggest one of them who did it. Why do you not ask them, if they can speak properly?"

At this, the idol-worshippers felt ashamed. "You know very well that they cannot speak," they told Ibrahim. "Do you then worship things that can neither be of any good to you nor do you any harm?" Ibrahim asked.

At this, the people became angrier than ever. In revenge, they threw Ibrahim into a fire. Ibrahim

might have been badly burned, perhaps killed. But he had Allah's help. Allah made the fire cool so that Ibrahim was not burned at all.

Later, Ibrahim left these idolatrous people and went to another country. When he was an old man, he had two sons, Ismail and Ishaq. Both of them were good and just men, and both were prophets of Allah. Ishaq's son, Yaqub, was also a prophet. So you can see that Ibrahim and his children were greatly blessed by Allah.

But first, Ibrahim had to endure a great test. An angel came to him and said: You have to sacrifice your only son. Ibrahim became very sad at this, but all the same, he knew that Allah had given him an order and he had to obey it. But first of all, he asked his son if he would agree. The son was good and pious, and he consoled his father: Dear father, he said calmly, if Allah has ordered it, then you must obey, so sacrifice me. Do not fear: with the help of Allah, I shall be brave.

So, full of sorrow, Ibrahim prepared to kill his son. But before he actually did so, he heard a voice: You have shown your good intentions, the voice told Ibrahim, this is sufficient. You have already fulfilled Allah's will.

Thus Ibrahim's son was saved, and Ibrahim understood that Allah had been testing him. Of course, Ibrahim was overcome with joy that he would not have to kill his son. They both thanked Allah and sacrificed instead an animal, as Allah had ordered.

To remember this occasion we Muslims celebrate every year and like Ibrahim and his son, we sacrifice an animal. This reminds us that Allah put Ibrahim to a test to see whether he would really obey him. Prophet Ibrahim passed the test and we celebrate in remembrance of this. Like Prophet Ibrahim, we also share the meat of the sacrificed animal with the poor people and our friends. On this occasion, we also thank Allah for everything that He has given us and for the lesson He taught us through the rescue of Ibrahim's son.

Later, Ibrahim and his son Ismail built the Ka'ba in Makka, and then they both prayed: O Allah, take this house in Your grace and help us and the people who come to us to be truly good Muslims.

Allah heard this prayer, and blessed the Ka'ba and the town of Makka. To this day, Muslims all over the world turn and face in the direction of the Ka'ba in Makka when they are praying. Muslims from all over the world come to the Ka'ba during the pilgrimage season. They come on foot, on camels, by car and aeroplanes. The Ka'ba is the oldest prayer house of Allah on earth. It is at the Ka'ba that all Muslims worship Allah together, and that includes all those who lived earlier, all those who are living now and all those who will live in the future.

9. Prophet Lut

(Lot)

Prophet Lut and his family lived among very evil and disobedient people. These people did many things which Allah had forbidden. So Allah commanded Lut to tell them: You must stop doing evil and believe in Allah. Allah has sent me to warn you of a terrible punishment that is going to befall you if you do not obey Him.

But people refused to listen to Lut. They even laughed at him because he would not join them in doing evil deeds.

One day, some visitors came to Lut. The evil people wanted to capture his visitors and harm them. Lut was very afraid that he would not be able to protect his guests. But to Lut's surprise and relief, the visitors said: You need not be frightened. Those evil-doers cannot harm us. For we are messengers of Allah. We have come from Allah to tell you to take your family and leave this town at night. None of you should try to turn and look back or stay behind. Only those who go without looking back will be saved.

Lut knew at once that the visitors were indeed Allah's angels. They had come so that Lut and his family could escape and be safe, for Allah was going to punish the evil-doers of that town. Lut and his family, however, had believed in Allah and prayed to Him. Therefore they were to be saved.

At once, Lut and his family got ready and left their house at night when it was dark, so that the evil people would not see them. But then, just as they were leaving, Lut's wife turned back and stayed behind. She refused to believe in Allah and was also disobedient. So she was not saved from punishment and death when Allah sent down a rain of fire and stones. All the houses in the town were destroyed and the disobedient people perished in the rain of fire and stones.

Only Lut and the rest of his family were rescued, and they praised and thanked Allah for having saved them.

10. Prophet Shu'aib

(Jethro)

Allah has sent a prophet to every people. Prophet Shu'aib was sent to the people of Madyan. These people, who were merchants and traders, were also called forest dwellers because they lived near a thick forest.

Shu'aib said to them: You should pray to Allah Who has created you. You should not cheat other people who come to buy from you.

But the forest dwellers did not listen to Shu'aib. They wanted to earn more money, and they earned more by cheating their customers. So they went on doing it. What was more, they refused to believe what Shu'aib told them. Get out of our town or we will throw stones at you, the forest dwellers threatened. If what you say is true, then we would have been punished long ago. We don't believe you and we are not going to worship Allah. We are not afraid of His punishment.

It did not take long for Allah's punishment to come to them. They all died in one day from a terrible earthquake. The large amounts of money which they had gained and collected could not help them at all. So their cheating was punished and it had done them no good at all to demand high prices and get rich quickly.

When the town was destroyed, Shu'aib and his companions who believed in Allah were saved. As the forest dwellers died, Shu'aib said to them: I have always reminded you to pray to Allah and I have warned you not to cheat other people. Now Allah has punished you!

11. Prophet Yusuf
(Joseph)

Yusuf had eleven brothers. Ten were older than him, and one was younger. Yusuf was a very good and handsome boy and his father Yaqub loved him very much. Unfortunately, this made his eleven brothers jealous, so they decided to get rid of Yusuf. One day, they took Yusuf to a deep well and threw him into it. Then, they took Yusuf's shirt and soaked it in sheep's blood. They showed the shirt to their father and said to him, "Our brother Yusuf is dead. A wolf has eaten him."

At this Yaqub was overcome with grief, and he wept bitterly for his beloved son. Years passed, and Yaqub became old and blind. But his trust in Allah remained firm and unswerving. Yaqub prayed very hard to Allah and never gave up hope that Yusuf was still alive and that one day they would be together again. Yaqub was certain this would be so. Yaqub was right, for when Yusuf had found himself in the well, he, too, had prayed to Allah. A caravan with merchants came and passed by the well. They found Yusuf, pulled him out and took him with them to Egypt. There he was sold in the market place to a man and his wife, who had no children of their own.

Sometimes it happens in life that a person is unjustly accused of a crime he did not commit. This is what happened to Yusuf when he grew up to be a man. He was put into prison, even though he had not done anything wrong. Only Allah knows best what is good for man, and He helps those who have faith in Him.

Years later, while Yusuf was still in prison, the Pharaoh of Egypt had a dream which caused him much concern. "I see seven fat cows who are being eaten by seven thin ones, and seven green ears of corn and seven dried ones", he told his courtiers. But none of the courtiers could explain what this dream meant. Then Pharaoh learned that the imprisoned Yusuf knew how to interpret it. So, Pharaoh sent for Yusuf and Yusuf explained: your dream means that the first seven years to come will be good years with good harvest, but the next seven years to follow will be bad years with famine and hunger. Therefore, you should collect and save as much grain as you can from the first good years and store it for the time of hunger!

The Pharaoh was very grateful to Yusuf and requested his help in overcoming the famine, for he realized that Yusuf was a wise and capable man. Yusuf agreed, and the Pharaoh made him treasurer and inspector of Egypt's storage chambers.

When the famine came and spread over the country, it also affected the people in Yusuf's own land. They too became hungry and during this time, Yusuf's brothers arrived in Egypt. They wanted to buy grain from the plentiful supply which Yusuf had told the Egyptians to store. Allah planned that when they reached Egypt, the brothers would come before Yusuf. At first they did not recognise him, for they thought that he was long dead. Later on, though, they realised who Yusuf was and felt very ashamed of what they had done all those years ago. They begged Yusuf's pardon and Yusuf forgave them. "Bring our father to me", Yusuf said to his brothers.

When the brothers brought their father to Yusuf, the old man was full of happiness. He had always believed that Yusuf was still alive and had never stopped praying to Allah. Father and son embraced each other. It was a wonderful reunion for them after such a long time apart.

Afterwards, Yusuf's father and brothers remained in Egypt. They grew into a big family and raised many children. And in the story of Musa, you will learn what became of these children.

Yusuf, who was a good, noble man and a prophet of Allah, had always told the Egyptians: you should worship only Allah. Allah has created you and protected and preserved you from hunger. You must be grateful to Allah and do good deeds.

12. Prophet Ayyub
(Job)

Prophet Ayyub lived a very long time ago. He was a very wealthy man with a large family. Then one misfortune after another came over him: he lost all his wealth, his family died, and eventually he also became very ill.

In his misery he prayed to Allah. In spite of his problems and worries he had no doubts. He trusted in Allah.

And Allah did help Ayyub. While he was sick and lonely, Allah told him to kick hard with his foot. Thereupon fresh water gushed out from the ground. With it Ayyub was able to refresh and wash himself and he also drank from it. That was how he regained his strength.

Because Ayyub firmly believed in Allah and remembered Him, Allah rewarded him very generously. Allah gave Ayyub a family again, which was twice as large as the first, and He also gave him a double amount of prosperity in money, servants and livestock. In the end Ayyub lived a long life with his children and grandchildren.

In this way Allah helped Prophet Ayyub, because even in his great misfortune he never failed to trust in Allah. People should draw a lesson from it that they should pray only to Allah when they are grieved and worried.

13. Prophet Musa
(Moses)

In the land of Egypt where the children of Ibrahim, Yaqub and Yusuf once lived, there reigned an evil, wicked Pharaoh. One day, this wicked Pharaoh ordered that all boys decended from Yusuf should be killed. He gave this order because he did not want Yusuf's children to increase and become more powerful than his own people.

It was at this dangerous time that the baby Musa was born. Allah sent a message to his mother, telling her to place little Musa in a small basket and put the basket on the river. That way, Musa would escape the dreadful fate which Pharaoh had decreed.

The basket with the little child in it was found by the Pharaoh's wife. She was kind and good-hearted and took Musa into the palace. Nobody knew who his parents were, but the Pharaoh's wife wanted to keep him, so she looked for a foster mother to nurse him. Allah then caused Musa's own mother to be brought into the palace so that she could be chosen as Musa's foster mother. So the baby Musa's life was saved, and through the help of Allah, he was given back to his own mother.

Musa was brought up in Pharaoh's palace and had the best teachers to educate him. They made a clever and capable man out of him.

As Musa grew up to be a man, he had to leave Pharaoh's land on a journey. On the way, he passed by a well where the shepherds gave water to their sheep. Musa found there two women who also wanted to give their sheep water to drink. But they could not reach the water before the shepherds had taken their flocks away from the well. Musa helped them to give water to their herd and when the two women returned home, they told their old father what had happened. He sent one of them back to invite Musa to come to their house. Later the father offered him one of his daughters to take for his wife, and Musa accepted. Afterwards, Musa led a happy life with his family and the old father by the well.

Some years later, Musa and his family were travelling in the country, when suddenly, he saw a big fire. He told his family to stay where they were and went on his own to find out about the fire. As Musa approached, he heard a voice: O Musa! the voice said, I am Allah, your Lord. I am going to make you my Prophet. You must go to the people and tell them that there is only one God, Allah, Who created them. So they must be grateful and pray only to Allah and strive to do good. Take your brother Harun with you and go to the Pharaoh and his people and give them My message.

Musa went to Egypt and told Pharaoh: Allah, Who is the Lord of the worlds, has sent me to you. I am Allah's messenger and I bring the truth to you. You should set free the children of Yusuf, who are being oppressed in this land, and let them come away with me.

When Pharaoh heard this, he became furious and shouted: You lie! No-one except I, the great Pharaoh of Egypt, is the lord of the world. I am the most powerful king on earth. You must be out of your mind to dare to say otherwise. If you disobey me, I will throw you into prison!

But Musa was not frightened by Pharaoh's anger or his words. With the help of Allah I shall show you

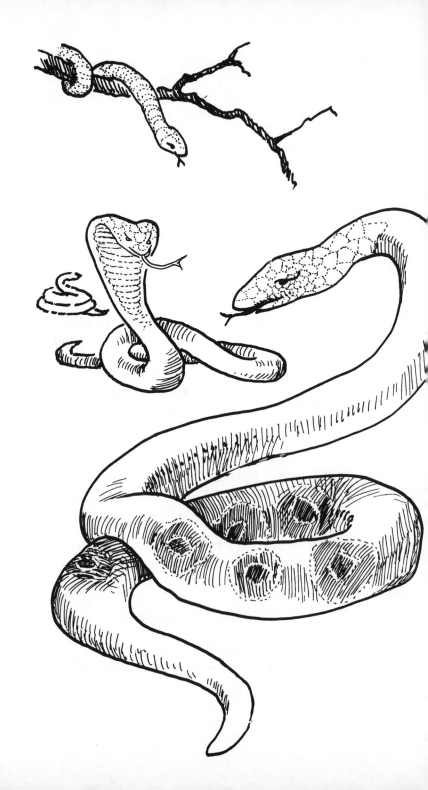

that Allah is more powerful than all men and also more powerful than you, he told the Pharaoh. Musa then took his stick and threw it onto the ground. At once, the stick turned into a long thick curling snake.

You are obviously a magician, said the Pharaoh when he saw this. I will call together all the magicians in my land, and then we will see who can make better magic, they or you.

So, all the magicians were summoned to the Pharaoh's palace. They had many sticks with them, and they turned them into snakes. But then Musa threw his stick once more onto the ground, and once more it turned into a snake. This snake swallowed up all the snakes which the magicians had made.

The magicians were impressed: We believe truly in Allah, Who has sent Musa as His prophet, they said, Allah is really and truly much more powerful than all or any of us.

The Pharaoh was furious. He said: Do you want to believe in something before I give you permission to believe it? You will all have your hands and feet chopped off as punishment! he shouted at the magicians.

Do you want to take revenge on us just because we believe in Allah's signs? the magicians replied. Whatever you do to us, we will still turn to Allah. May Allah have mercy on us and help us to be patient and steadfast. In this way the magicians, who were greedy men, were turned into good and faithful servants of Allah.

Now Musa went to the descendants of Yusuf who were suffering much oppression under the rule of the evil Pharaoh. He told them: We shall go away from Egypt. But after they had departed, Pharaoh and his soldiers went after them to fetch them back.

Musa and his people sped on their journey until

they finally reached the sea. By this time, though, Pharaoh and his soldiers were approaching and the people grew terribly afraid. But Allah came to their rescue. He divided the water into two, so that Musa and his people could walk through the middle to get across the sea. When Pharaoh and his soldiers reached the sea, they of course rode after them. But they could not reach Musa and his people before they came to the other side. Suddenly, while Pharaoh and his soldiers were still riding across the sea bed, the waters came flowing back, and all of them were drowned. Allah had thus saved Musa and his people because they worshipped Him alone. Pharaoh, who refused to believe in Allah and who was proud and even wanted to throw Musa into prison, was left to drown.

After their escape, Musa and his people wandered in the desert for many years. One day, Musa received Allah's order to climb a high mountain. Musa was to stay there for forty days and nights praying to Allah and listening to what Allah would tell him and his people. But forty days and nights seemed a long time and while Musa was away, his people became impatient. They decided to make a calf out of gold and worship it. When Musa came down from the mountain, he saw the calf and became very angry. He smashed the calf into a thousand pieces and scolded his people so much that they felt ashamed of themselves. You must never, ever worship anything else apart from Allah, Musa instructed them.

Musa had brought a book to his people which Allah had revealed to him on the mountain. This book is called the Taurat. In the Taurat, it is stated what men should do and what they should not do. They must never worship anything else apart from Allah.

63

They must never kill a fellow man. They must not take things which do not belong to them. They must be good to their parents and to one another.

Musa's people understood now that they had been very ungrateful to Allah, for it was Allah who had saved them from Pharaoh and his soldiers. They prayed to Allah and thanked Him for what He had done for them. They asked for His forgiveness and made a promise that they would strive hard to do good deeds.

Allah forgives those who are ashamed for the bad deeds they have done, and are willing to correct their mistakes and return to Allah.

14. Prophet Yunus

(Jonah)

Prophet Yunus was sent by Allah to a big town where the people had forgotten Allah's orders and did many things which Allah had forbidden. You should believe only in Allah and obey only Him, Yunus told them. You should worship Him alone and do good, otherwise a severe punishment will come upon you!

But Yunus soon discovered that the people did not want to listen to him. He lost patience with them and left the town in anger. Afterwards, Yunus decided to go across the sea, and boarded a ship for the voyage. But when the ship was in the middle of the ocean, Yunus suffered a great misfortune. He was thrown overboard and swallowed up by an enormous fish. Fortunately, though, the fish had swallowed Yunus in one big gulp, so he landed in its stomach unhurt.

It was very dark inside the fish's stomach, and Yunus grew very fearful. In his loneliness, he started to think over what had happened in the town, and came to realize that he should not have acted so hastily and in such a quick-tempered manner. Instead, he should have stayed and kept on speaking to the people and ask them to return to Allah.

In his despair, Yunus started to pray with all his heart to Allah. He said: '' O Allah, there is no God apart from You. You alone do I praise and honour. I have done wrong; if You do not help me, I shall be lost for ever.''

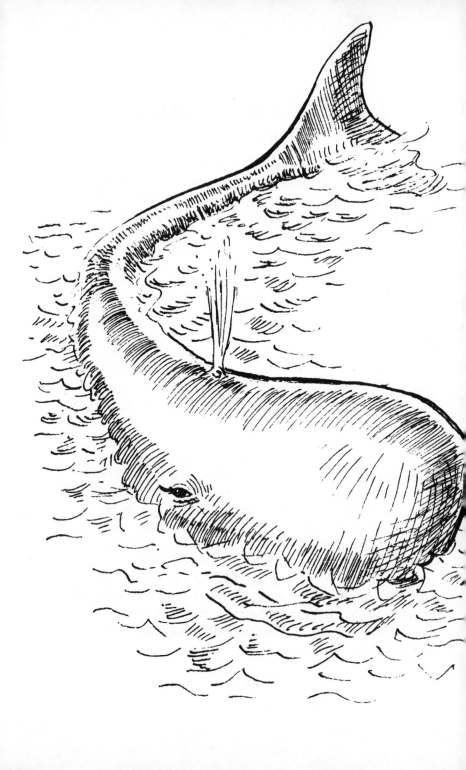

Allah hears the prayers of those who pray to Him and those who believe in Him. Allah heard Yunus's prayer, and He caused Yunus to come out of the fish's stomach, and to be swept by the waves of the sea onto the shore. Poor Yunus was in a terrible state and lay on the shore, weak, ill and helpless. He felt dreadfully miserable, but Allah caused a tree to grow and this tree provided Yunus with shade and nourishing fruits. Before long, Yunus had recovered his health and strength.

When he was better, Allah sent Yunus back to the town. This time, though, the people there listened to Yunus when he told them: You should believe in Allah and worship Him alone. You must do good.

67

15. Prophet Dawud
(David)

When Dawud was young, he was a shepherd boy. He was also very strong and courageous. Once, a troop of fierce warriors came to attack his people. Among them was Jalut. Everybody had a great fear of Jalut, and no-one was willing to fight against him except for Dawud. Dawud challenged Jalut to a combat and killed him. This so frightened the enemies of Dawud's people that they fled as fast as they could. Dawud was very brave, of course, but Allah had helped him triumph over the mighty Jalut. Allah also gave Dawud wisdom, power and skills. Dawud was a very clever smith and made wonderful things out of iron, like weapons and armour.

Dawud could also sing very well. He sang to praise and honour Allah. These songs, which Dawud had learned from the angels, were written down in a book called Zabur. Allah had revealed this book, Zabur, to Dawud, just as He had revealed to Musa the book which is called Taurat.

Allah made Dawud His prophet and the ruler over his people. He was a very just ruler and his people always came to him when they had quarrels with each other. Once, some sheep had wandered off during the night into somebody else's field and ate up all the crops. Dawud decided that as punishment, the sheep must be given to the owner of the field who had lost all his crops.

When Sulaiman, the son of Dawud, heard that, he protested: But the field is still there. It is only this

year's harvest that is gone. So surely the sheep should not be completely taken away from their owner. The owner should have them back as soon as the loss of harvest is recovered.

Dawud agreed with the good advice of his son Sulaiman, and decided to settle the problem as Sulaiman had suggested.

In the next story, you will hear about Sulaiman, who was also chosen by Allah to be His prophet.

Dawud, who was Allah's prophet, always said to his people: You should believe in Allah and worship Him alone and do good.

16. Prophet Sulaiman
(Solomon)

Sulaiman was the son of Dawud. As you already know, Sulaiman was very just even as a young boy, and he became well known and respected for his wisdom. When he became a man, Allah made him His prophet. Allah also taught him to understand the languages of birds and animals. Yet in spite of his wisdom and many wealthy possessions, Sulaiman never forgot Allah. He knew that all goodness comes from Allah. Thus, he always told his people: Thank Allah for the good He has given you and for His generosity. Worship Allah and do good deeds.

Once, Sulaiman and his soldiers were passing through a valley inhabited by ants. Sulaiman heard one ant say to another: Quick, get out of the way and hide! Sulaiman and his soldiers are coming, and they will trample on us and not even know they have done so!

Sulaiman, of course, was able to understand the ants' language. He laughed and ordered his soldiers to stay still and wait until all the ants had crawled away to safety. Then he prayed to Allah: O Allah, help me in doing the right things so that You will be contented with me.

One day, Sulaiman called all the birds to gather round him, but as he glanced through the flock, he noticed that the Hoopoe bird was not there. Sulaiman waited for some time, and just as he was deciding not to wait any longer, the Hoopoe suddenly came flying in and sat himself down next to

Sulaiman. I have come from a far-away city called Saba, the Hoopoe said. The people there are very rich and they have a Queen who sits on a magnificent throne. These people worship the sun and believe that they are right to treat the sun as God. But they are wrong, are they not? They will never find the right way to Allah if they go on like that. Allah is the only One Whom all creatures should worship.

Sulaiman then wrote a letter to the Queen of Saba and sent the Hoopoe to take it to her.

When the Queen of Saba received the letter, she called all the wise men of the city to her. I have received a letter from Sulaiman, said the Queen. In it, Sulaiman writes that we should believe in Allah and worship only Him. What would you advise me to do?

We are very powerful and can make war against Sulaiman, but you have to decide yourself what is to be done, the wise men answered.

But a war could cause destruction to our city, and our best warriors will turn into cruel fighters, the Queen protested. Therefore, I would prefer not to make war. Instead, I will send Sulaiman a present.

When the messengers of the Queen of Saba arrived with the present, they were very surprised because Sulaiman became very angry. Why do you bring me these riches instead of listening to my advice? Sulaiman scolded. What Allah has given me is much better than all these riches. Go to your Queen and take her presents with you!

When she heard that Sulaiman had refused her valuable gifts, the Queen of Saba, in her turn, was surprised. So, she decided to go to see Sulaiman for herself. She called her people and made preparations for the journey to Sulaiman's city.

When the Queen arrived, Sulaiman explained to

her about Allah and she realized how wrong she had been to worship the sun. You are right, she told Sulaiman, from now on, I shall worship only Allah. He is our only Lord and we should obey only Him.

17. Prophet Zakariya and Prophet Yahya
(Zacharias and John)

Zakariya and his wife were very old, and to their sorrow they did not have any children. They wanted very much to have a son, so Zakariya prayed to Allah: Let my wife and I have a son before we die.

As Zakariya was saying his prayer, an angel of Allah appeared. You have prayed to Allah and Allah has heard your prayer, the angel told him. Your wife will have a son and his name will be Yahya. He will be a good and honourable man and he will be Allah's prophet.

Even though Zakariya had prayed for this, he was surprised: But my wife and I are very old! he said. How can we have a son?

When Allah has willed a thing, it will happen, the angel assured him. As a sign that you are going to have a son, you must not speak to anyone for three days.

So it happened that even when Zakariya wanted to speak to someone, he could not move his tongue. Only after three days was he able to speak again. He knew then that they were going to have a son. Both he and his wife were very happy. They prayed to Allah and thanked Him, and when the son was born, they named him Yahya.

Yahya was a good and loving son. He prayed to Allah together with his father Zakariya and his mother. The three of them always did good deeds. Yahya was very kind and good to all people and all animals. He was never proud or bad-tempered, and

Allah made him His prophet. Yahya was a pious and humble servant of Allah and he always told people to pray to Allah because Allah had created mankind.

Allah's blessing for Yahya can be found in the Qur'an: ''Peace was with him on the day he was born and on the day he died, and peace will be with him on the day when he will come to life again.''

Whoever is as good and pious as Prophet Yahya will be blessed with everlasting peace by Allah.

بِسْمِ اللهِ الرَّحْمٰنِ الرَّحِيْمِ

اِنَّآ اَعْطَيْنٰكَ الْكَوْثَرَ ۝١

فَصَلِّ لِرَبِّكَ وَانْحَرْ ۝٢

اِنَّ شَانِئَكَ هُوَ الْاَبْتَرُ ۝٣

AL-KAUTHAR

Bismi-llahi-r-rahmani-r-rahim
Inna a'tainaka-l-kauthar
Fasalli li-rabbika wa-nhar
Inna shani'aka huwa-labtar

AL-KAUTHAR

In the Name of Allah, the Merciful, the Mercy-giving.
Indeed, We have given you abundance
So pray to your Lord and make sacrifice.
Indeed, you enemy is the one cut-off.

18. Prophet Isa

(Jesus)

The mother of Prophet Isa was called Maryam. Some people also call her Mary. She was a very pious woman and once, an angel of Allah came to her and said: Soon you will have a son. But how can I have a son? Maryam asked. I have no husband. The angel replied: Allah is almighty. When He wishes something, then it will happen. You will have a son, and his name shall be Isa, and he will be a great prophet of Allah.

When Isa was born, Maryam was on her own. She was very sad and hungry, for she had nothing to eat. But Allah came to her aid. He made a stream flow and a tree with nourishing fruits grew in the place where Maryam lived. Now, she would not have to suffer thirst and hunger.

Later Maryam returned to her family. They were very curious about the child and asked: How did you get him?

But Maryam did not answer. Instead, she just pointed to the child. Don't be silly, Maryam! the people admonished her. How can we ask a child, who is still in the cradle?

But just then, to their amazement, they heard the child say: I am the servant of Allah. He has given me the scripture and made me His prophet. We, mankind, should worship only Allah and help the poor and give them some of our money.

Years passed and Isa grew to be a man. Often, he spoke to the people and told them what Allah had revealed to him. He told them too of the earlier prophets of Allah. He told them: I am also a prophet of Allah and I am also a man like all the other prophets of Allah. You should believe in Allah and worship no-one apart from Allah. You should be good to one another and help each other.

Some people have given Isa the name Jesus. They say that Allah is the father of Jesus. We know that this is not true. Isa himself has said that he is only a prophet of Allah, even though he had no father. Allah has no sons. Only human beings have sons and daughters.

Isa brought a book to mankind. This book is called Injil, and Allah gave this book to Isa. In it there are many stories and it is also stated there that mankind should worship only Allah.

Prophet Isa had many blessings from Allah. He was able to perform many miracles with Allah's help. He could cure the sick so that they would be grateful to Allah and obey and pray to Allah alone. Isa could also bring the dead back to life so that the people would be happy and pray to Allah and thank Him.

Prophet Isa told the people of another prophet who was going to come later, whose name would be Prophet Ahmad. It was Allah who had sent Prophet Isa to the people to tell them that Prophet Muhammad would come.

There were many people who listened to Prophet Isa and worshipped Allah, but there were some who refused to listen and wanted to kill him. Evil people have always tried to persecute and kill Allah's prophets. We know that from the stories of Ibrahim and Yusuf and many other prophets.

But when the evil people were just about to kill Isa, Allah came to his rescue, just as He had rescued other prophets when they were in danger.

Some people say that Prophet Isa was nailed onto a cross by his enemies and that he died in this way. But we know this is not true. Allah protected Prophet Isa so that the people could not carry out their evil intentions. Allah said to Isa: I will let you die in peace and then you will come to Me and be with Me. Those who had been following you and prayed to Me and did good will be brought to Me. They will receive the best rewards, because they have been very obedient.

Thus Allah helps His prophets when they are in danger, and He also helps those who follow the prophets and worship only Allah and do good.

19. The Last Prophet

You have already heard about Prophet Muhammad. Adam was the first prophet and Muhammad was the last prophet. Allah had given Muhammad a book, which is called the Qur'an. All the stories about the prophets which you have now read can be found in the Qur'an. In the Qur'an is also written what you should do and what you are not allowed to do.

Muhammad was the last prophet because Allah gave him the Qur'an and all that we must know about Allah can be found in the Qur'an. Everybody can look in the Qur'an to discover what he should do. Therefore, there is no need for another prophet after Muhammad.

Muhammad, like the other prophets, told the people: You should worship only Allah. Allah has created you, He has made plants and animals so that you can eat of them. He made the earth, sky, water, air and the day and the night for you. So be grateful to Him and do good.

Now you know the stories of many prophets. But remember that there are more prophets in addition to these, for Allah has sent His prophets to all peoples. You must also have noticed that all the prophets had been saying the same thing: Mankind should worship only Allah. Prophet Muhammad has taught us how we should worship Allah. You can also learn it: it is not difficult.

There are, however, other things that we should do. We must believe in Allah, we must pray, fast, share our money with the poor and needy, and go on a pilgrimage to Makka once in our lifetime, if we can afford it. You will learn more about all this later in this book.

20. Resurrection and the Day of Judgement

As you know, Allah always sent prophets to mankind. These prophets told man what is good and what is bad. The prophets have also told many other things. They said: When we die, we will be buried, but Allah is Almighty. He will wake us all from death. This will happen on the Day of Resurrection. On this day, all of us will be gathered to Allah. Those of us who have done good will remain with Allah for ever. But those who have done evil, and have not repented, or asked Allah's forgiveness, will not be allowed to remain with Allah. Such is the Day of Judgement. To strive to do good means to listen to the words of the prophets and thus obey Allah. In this way, one can always remain with Allah after death. But to turn to evil means not to listen to the word of the prophets and to disobey Allah. Therefore those who do evil may not remain with Allah after they are dead.

So you may ask, why doesn't everybody want to do good? The reason is that some people think they don't have to listen to the prophets. But they are wrong to think so: The prophets have told people what they should do. We should do good as long as we live. Doing good brings more happiness in life than anything else. We shall have friends who are good people and we shall have these friends for as long as we live, and after we die.

However, the people who do evil will have evil people with them. They will have many enemies.

They will have enemies all their life and when they die, too.

The prophets and the people who worship Allah are our friends. The people who do evil and who turn away from Allah are not our friends.

21. Our Beliefs

We believe in Allah, the one and only almighty God, Lord and Creator. Him we trust and Him alone we fear.

We believe in the angels created by Allah. We know them even though they are not visible to us. They are the obedient servants of Allah and they carry out all His orders.

We believe that the words which Allah revealed to the prophets were written down in books. The last book, which was given to Muhammad is the Qur'an. The Qur'an is the only book from Allah which is complete and preserved in its original form.

We believe that Allah has sent His prophets to all mankind with the message to worship only Allah and to do good.

We believe in the Day of Resurrection when Allah will wake us from our deaths. We will be rewarded for the good that we have done and those of us who did not believe in Allah and did evil, will be punished.

We believe that Allah has taught us to understand what good and evil is, so that we can ourselves decide for the good and against the evil.

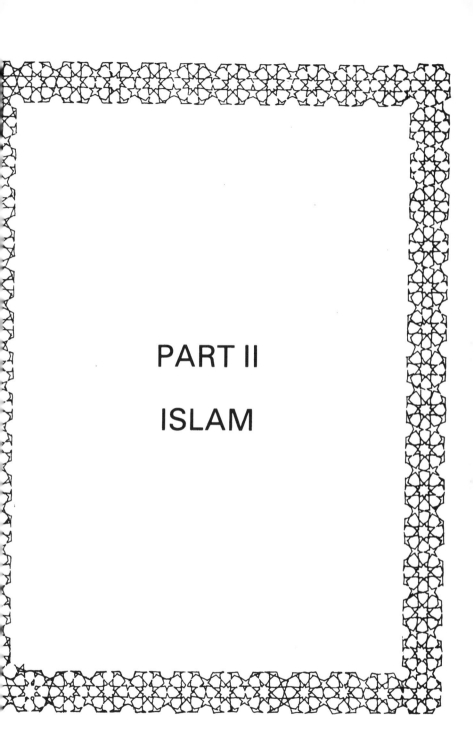

PART II

ISLAM

1. Shahada

Hasan and Laila are brother and sister and their parents brought them to live in this country. Often they have heard adults talking about Prophet Muhammad and Islam. They have also heard them say: "We are Muslims". This made the children curious. Once Hasan asked his father, "What does it mean when you say we are Muslims?"

His father replied, "It means we follow the words of Allah which were brought to Prophet Muhammad by the angel Gabriel and which are recorded in the Holy Qur'an."

Hasan and Laila had already heard something of the Qur'an and the angel Gabriel.

"What is Islam?" asked Laila.

"Islam is our faith" said her father, "A Muslim who follows Islam does five things: he says the Shahada, he prays five times a day, he fasts for a month in Ramadan, he gives Zakat to the poor and he goes on a pilgrimage to Makka when he has saved enough money to make the journey."

"That sounds like a lot of things to do," Hasan and Laila commented.

"Well," said their father, "you don't have to learn it all at once, but if you spend some time on it each day, then you will be able to fulfil all the five duties, like all other good Muslims. To say the Shahada, to pray five times daily, to fast in Ramadan, to give Zakat and to go at least once in a lifetime on a pilgrimage to Makka."

لا إله إلا الله

محمد رسول الله

"There is something I still don't understand," said Hasan, "What is Shahada?"

Father smiled and told Hasan, "Do not worry. There are some things that you don't understand yet, but you will soon learn them. Laila too. Today we will start with the Shahada. Now," Father said, "Say after me: Ashhadu an la ilaha illa llah."

Hasan repeated it with his father. "Ashhadu an la ilaha illa llah."

"I know it already!" exclaimed Laila, "Ashhadu an la ilaha illa llah."

"That's right," said Father, "but you must also know what it means. It means: I bear witness that there is no god apart from Allah. Ashhadu an la ilaha illa llah. When you say that you are saying the Shahada. We Muslims know that Allah is God and that there are no other gods apart from Him. It is Allah Who has created us and the whole world. Allah has created everything that is there. That is what we mean when we say: la ilaha illa llah. These words mean "There is no god apart from Allah" in the Arabic language as Prophet Muhammad has taught us."

"That's not very difficult," said Hasan.

"Of course it isn't!" said Father, "but we are not finished yet. That is only the first part of the Shahada."

"What is the second part like?" asked Laila curiously.

Father said it very slowly: "Wa ashhadu anna Muhammada-rasulu-llah."

"Please say both the parts of the Shahada together again," requested Laila.

"Gladly," said Father, "Ashhadu an la ilaha illa llah wa ashhadu anna Muhammada-rasulu-llah."

Laila tried it first. "Ash... Ash... Ash..." But she

90

stumbled over the words and could go no further.

"Ashhadu!" exclaimed Hasan.

Laila continued: "Ashhadu an la ilaha illa llah wa ashhadu anna Muhammada-rasulu-llah."

"Right!" said Father, "Now it is your turn, Hasan!"

Hasan said the Shahada without any mistakes.

"Now you also have to know what it means in English. It means: I bear witness that there is no god apart from Allah and I bear witness that Muhammad is the messenger of Allah."

أشهد أن لا اله الا الله
وأشهد أن محـمدًا رسول الله

2. Washing for Prayer

Once, Laila asked her mother, "How did the people learn how they were supposed to pray?"

Her mother answered, "Prophet Muhammad showed them."

"I would like to pray, too," said Laila, "would you show me how?"

"Of course I will," said her mother, "I'll show you and I'll also tell you how Prophet Muhammad showed it to the people. You will soon know how it is done. All Muslims pray in the same way, just as the Prophet has said, so that they are able to pray together at the same time. Otherwise, each will be doing it in a different way. We also say the prayer in Arabic so that all will be saying the same thing and not each saying it differently. We want to be able to pray together, but if one is saying it in Arabic and the other in Urdu and another in English, then it would be impossible. Therefore we say our prayers in Arabic, just as Prophet Muhammad has instructed us.

"Prophet Muhammad has said that we should wash ourselves before praying so that we would be clean," Laila's mother continued, "It is as if by washing ourselves with clean, clear water we are also washing away our unclean thoughts. It is not good to be unclean when praying."

"Now I will show you how to wash," said Mother, "First, we wash our hands with water, then we rinse mouth and nose and wash the face. Next, we wash our arms, the right one first and then the left,

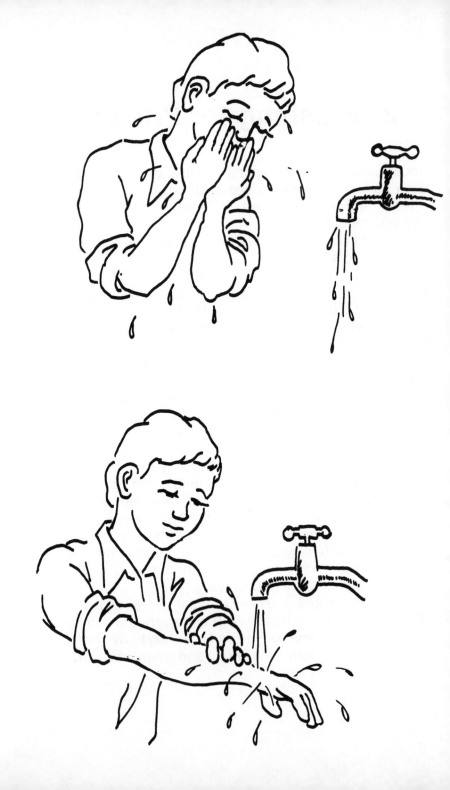

starting from the elbows. When this is done we wet our head just by stroking the hair with our wet hands. Last but not least, we wash our feet, starting with the right foot and then the left. Now we are clean and ready for prayer.''

''That's quite easy, really,'' said Laila, ''First I wash my hands, then I rinse my mouth and nose, after that I wash my face, and then...'' Laila stopped. She could not remember what came next. She looked disappointed, but her mother smiled and told her: ''Do not worry, you almost know it all. After the face comes the arms, and do you know which one you wash first?''

''I know,'' said Laila, ''first the right and then the left, starting from my elbows, then with my wet hands I wet my hair by stroking it. Last of all I wash my feet, first the right and then the left, then I am clean.''

''What are the words of the prayer?'' Laila asked, ''I still haven't learned them yet.''

''No, not yet,'' agreed her mother, ''but the washing comes first and it is very important. I think that is enough for today. Tomorrow I'll show you how the Prophet has shown us the prayer.''

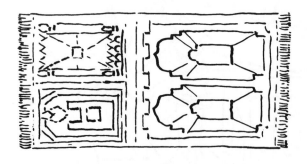

3. The Prayer

"Yesterday, you learned how to wash before prayer," Laila's mother told her. "Today I'll show you how to do the prayer. But before we start, show me how we wash. Do you still remember?"

"Of course I do!" said Laila, and she began to demonstrate it to her mother.

Her mother was pleased. "Very good," she said. "You have learned it quite quickly."

Laila was very happy at her mother's praise. Mother then went on to explain: "Prophet Muhammad said that we should stand in a neat row when we are praying together, otherwise there will be confusion. We stand in a position so that we are facing towards the direction of Makka."

"Why do we have to do that?" asked Laila.

"Because the Ka'ba is in Makka," Mother replied. "You know the Ka'ba is the oldest praying house of Allah. Allah has told us through Muhammad that we should face the Ka'ba when we pray. That is our Qibla, which is the direction towards which we pray. This is where all the good thoughts of all Muslims meet when they pray together. That is much better than having each Muslim facing somewhere else while praying, isn't it?"

"Oh yes," agreed Laila, "but tell me more. I want to know what it is like."

"Now don't hurry over it," said Mother. "You had better watch carefully so that you can remember it. After standing and facing towards Makka, we must

keep silent and concentrate. In our thoughts, we compose ourselves to pray and we ask Allah to help us pray correctly. Then we raise our hands up to our ears and say: Allahu akbar.''

"That means, Allah is great," interrupted Laila quickly. "I know that already."

Mother nodded and said: "Now we lay our hands, the right one over the left, and recite the Surah Al-Fatiha."

"I've learned that one, may I recite it?" asked Laila excitedly.

"Yes," said Mother, "but remember to keep facing towards Qibla and recite it properly."

Laila raised her hands and said: "Allahu akbar." Then she laid her hands down, the right over the left and began with the Surah Al-Fatiha:

"Bismi-llahi-rahmani-rahim.

Alhamdu-li-llahi rabbi-l-alamin. Ar-rahmani-rahim.

Maliki yaumi-din. Iyaka na'budu wa iyyaka nasta'in.

Ihdina-sirata-l-mustaqim. Sirata-ladhina an'amta alaihaim ghairi-l-maghdubi alaihim wa la dalin. Amin.''

"That's very good, Laila!" Mother told her. Laila was very happy. She was very anxious to learn the prayer and she enjoyed it because she already knew some of it.

"What comes next?" Laila wanted to know.

"Stay as you are," said Mother, "and say another short surah. You know what a surah is, don't you? It is a part of the Qur'an, and the Qur'an is the book which Allah revealed to Prophet Muhammad. Do you know a short surah?"

"Yes," said Laila, "the Surah Al-Ikhlas:

Qul huwa-llahu ahad. Allahu samad.

Lam yalid wa lam yulad

100

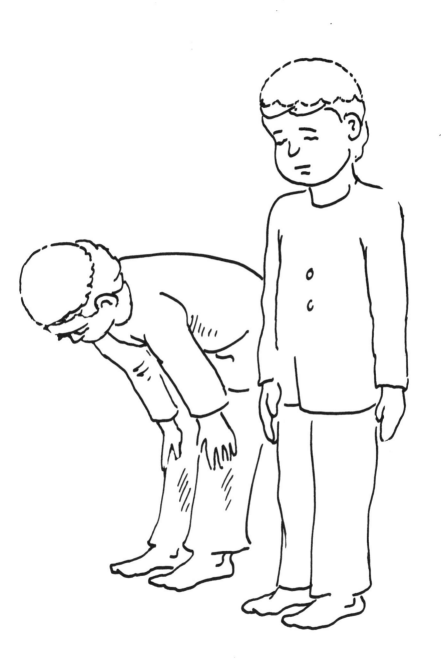

wa lam yaku-lahu kufuwan ahad.''

"That was very good,'' said Mother. "Already, you can recite two surahs by heart.''

"I know another one,'' cried Laila, "Inna ataina...''

Mother smiled and said, "Wait! Not so fast! You can recite that later.'' Mother went on to explain how Prophet Muhammad had said that after reciting Surah Al-Fatiha, we should recite another short surah. Then we should bow forward and repeat three times: Subhana-rabbi-al-azim.

"What does it mean?'' asked Laila.

"That means, Glory be to my Lord the most Great,'' answered Mother.

"That means my greatest Lord is Allah,'' said Laila and bowed forward saying three times, "Subhana rabbi-al-azim.''

Mother continued. "We then stand upright again and say: Sami'a-llahu liman hamida rabbana wa laka-l-hamd. This means, Allah hears those who praise Him. O our Lord, You do we praise.''

Laila repeated the words "Sami'a-llahu liman hamida rabbana wa laka-l-hamd.''

"Then we say 'Allahu akbar' and kneel down.''

Laila followed her mother closely as she was explaining the prayers and paid careful attention to all she said and did.

"We now touch the ground with our forehead and say three times: 'Subhana rabbi-al-a'la','' Mother told Laila.

Laila followed her mother and repeated "Subhana rabbi-al-a'la'' three times.

"We then say: 'Allahu akbar' and sit down again. We say 'Allahu akbar' and bend down again touching the ground with our forehead.

While our forehead is still touching the ground, we

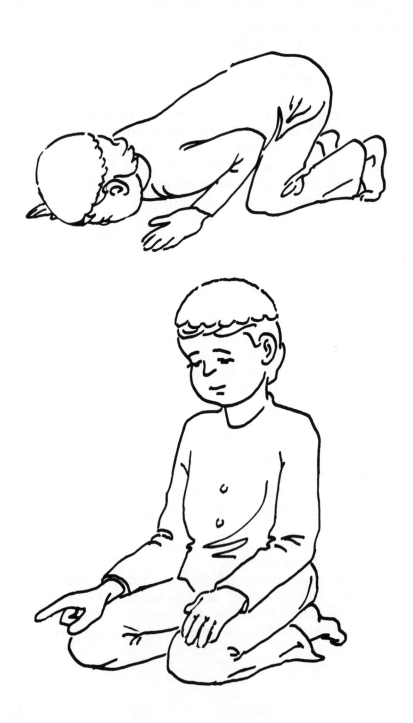

say three times: 'Subhana rabbi-al-a'la'.

Finally we stand upright again and while doing so, we say: 'Allahu akbar'.''

''But you have not yet told me what 'Subhana rabbi-al-a'la' means,'' said Laila.

''That means, Glory be to my Lord the most High,'' her mother answered. Mother was pleased. She knew now that Laila had been paying good attention.

''Well done,'' Mother praised, ''you have learned it beautifully. We shall practise it a few more times until you know it by heart, but for today, we have done enough. You have been very attentive and hard working and I am very proud of you. We shall learn more tomorrow and soon you will be able to pray just like an adult.''

Laila, too, was delighted that she had done everything correctly. Before going to bed, she tried to memorize the prayer words: Subhana rabbi-al-azim — that means, Glory be to my Lord the most great; Sami'a-llahu liman hamida — that means, Allah hears those who praise Him; and Subhana rabbi-al-a'la — that means, Glory be to my Lord the most High.

But Laila had done a lot of learning that day and she was tired. Before long, she was fast asleep.

4. The Prayer

(Second Part)

On the following day, Mother told Laila that the time had come for her to learn the second part of the prayer. "But before we start," Mother said, "let's go over what you have already learned."

Laila stood upright and said: "First of all I should stand in a position facing Makka, which is the Qibla."

"Right," said Mother, "but haven't you forgotten something, or have you already washed yourself?"

"Oh dear!" Laila exclaimed, "I did forget!"

Laila hurriedly ran to the bathroom and washed herself as her mother had taught her. She started off with her hands, then her mouth, nose, face, the arms from right to left, and then she wetted her hair with her fingers. When that was finished, she washed her feet, the right and then the left, right up to the ankles. As she was doing that, she thought to herself, "I had almost forgotten to wash before the prayer, even though I know how important it is. One must be clean for prayer. I must never forget again."

Then, she hurried back again to her mother and stood beside her on the praying mat. Laila concentrated her thoughts on the intention to carry out her prayer and faced Qibla. She raised both hands right up to the ears and said, "Allahu akbar." Then she laid her hands down, right over left, and started the prayer with the Surah Al-Fatiha and the short Surah Al-Ikhlas. She then said, "Allahu akbar", at the same time bending forward with hands on knees and repeated three times, "Subhana rabbi-al-azim". Then, standing upright again, she said "Sami'a-llahu liman hamida rabbana wa laka-l-hamd" and as she knelt down she said, "Allahu akbar." Then she touched the ground with her forehead, repeating three times "Subhana rabbi-al-a'la." After that she said "Allahu akbar" and sat upright again. Then she knelt down once more, saying thrice "Subhana rabbi-al-a'la."

Sometimes, Laila got stuck and faltered over the prayers, but her mother prompted her, and it all went well.

"Now you have just finished the first rak'a," said her mother. "You continue the second rak'a again with the Surah Al-Fatiha."

"Then the Surah Al-Ikhlas?" asked Laila.

"It would be better to recite another one, since you already know one," her mother suggested.

So, Laila recited the Surah Al-Kaussar:

Inna 'atainaka-l-kaussar.
Fasalli li rabbika wa-nhar.
Inna shani'aka huwa-l-abtar.

"Do I continue now just as the first rak'a?" asked Laila.

"Yes," said Mother, "Now we bow forward and say 'Subhana rabbi-al-azim'."

Laila bowed forward and then stood up again. Then when kneeling down, she said, "Subhana rabbi-al-a'la" and knelt once more and said, "Subhana rabbi-al-a'la."

"I've completed the second rak'a!" she exclaimed, very pleased.

"So you have!" said Mother, also very pleased. "The second rak'a is completed! Remember that the early morning prayer has just two rak'as. We end it with a few more words, and at the same time sit on

108

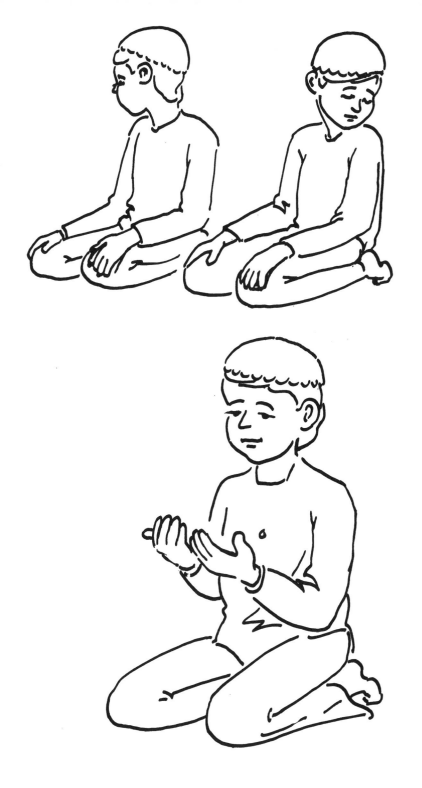

our heels.''

Laila sat on her heels and repeated after her mother:

"Ashhadu an la ilaha illa llah

wa ashhadu anna Muhammadan 'abduhu wa rasuluh''.

"That means: I bear witness that there is no god apart from Allah and I bear witness that Muhammad is His servant and messenger.''

"There is something else, though,'' Laila's mother told her. "Don't worry, you can always repeat after me when we pray together.'' Mother smiled. "It will not take you long to memorize it. This is how it goes:

"Allahumma salli 'ala Muhammad wa 'ala ali Muhammad. It means: O Allah, bless Muhammad and the followers of Muhammad.''

Laila then copied her mother, turning her face first to the right and then to the left, each time saying:

"As-salamu alaikum wa rahmatu-llah.''

"With that, we wish peace and Allah's blessing to everybody,'' explained Mother. Then she took Laila in her arms and hugged her, saying, "I am very proud of you because you already know how to pray. From now on we are going to do it every day together. Soon we will be able to surprise your father by showing him what a good, hard-working Muslim daughter he has!''

"Yes,'' said Laila, "but before that I shall have to learn the last bit, so that I can remember it and never forget it!''

"Make sure you also know the meaning of what you are memorizing,'' said Mother. "Even though we pray in Arabic like all other Muslims in the world, we still should know exactly what we are saying when we pray.'' As she was explaining that, she lovingly stroked Laila's hair.

Laila was very happy. She had managed to learn a lot in three days: how to wash for prayer and how to carry out the prayer itself. When she did it each day with her parents, she would know it by heart.

It was not difficult for her because her mother had explained it to her very clearly, just as Prophet Muhammad had once explained it to the Muslims in Makka and Medina. Those Muslims then explained it to their children, and so on in each generation. One day, Laila too would explain it to her own children, so that they would become good Muslims and know how to teach their own sons and daughters.

5. Fasting

Recently, Uncle Ismail arrived. It was only a short visit, for he could not stay long.

"The fasting month is about to begin," Uncle Ismail told Hasan and Laila, "and I would like to be home then."

"Tell us about the fasting month," said Hasan and Laila.

"Gladly," said Uncle Ismail, and he went on: "As soon as the fasting month begins, all Muslims in Pakistan, Arabia, Europe and all over the world start fasting. You can fast with the adults, but only for a few days. The whole month would be too long for you at the moment. But when you grow older, then it will be no problem."

"What is fasting?" asked Hasan.

"Fasting means not eating or drinking anything," answered Uncle Ismail.

"Nothing at all?" Hasan and Laila exclaimed.

"Absolutely nothing!" Uncle Ismail replied, but seeing their astonishment, he went on: "However, so that it will not be unbearable, we are allowed to break the fast at night. That means we fast in the month of Ramadan from early in the morning until the evening, when the sun sets."

"Why do we have to fast?" asked Laila.

"Well," said Uncle Ismail, "we learn many things through fasting, such as how well Allah has provided for us. Prophet Muhammad explained this to us. Allah has provided for us so that we have enough to

113

eat all the year round, without going hungry. Therefore the month of Ramadan is a reminder for us each year to be especially thankful to Allah for the nourishment He has given us. In other words, by fasting we learn to appreciate the value of the food which we often take for granted. If we don't eat during the day and we have to wait till evening, that makes us realize how good the food is."

Laila thought over what Uncle Ismail had said and she agreed with him. "I know that if I were to get as many sweets and candies every day as I wanted, and then not get any at all for a few days, that would make me think how much I like them," she remarked.

"That's right, Laila!" said Uncle Ismail. "But there are other reasons for fasting. When we fast, we learn to go through a day without eating. This is a very useful experience. For, if there were to come a day when you can't have anything to eat, you will not feel hungry so soon. So you will not panic because you know then that you have already withstood fasting during Ramadan. You will then be able to wait patiently till you get something to eat."

"You are right, Uncle!" said Hasan. "Once I forgot to take my sandwich when I went to school, and I was terribly hungry during the break. But if I were to start fasting and learn to bear it, I won't get so hungry the next time I forget my sandwich."

Uncle Ismail laughed. "That's true," he said, "but that is not all. There is still a better reason for fasting. When we don't eat, we can also feel how the poor people feel when they don't have anything to eat and come close to starving."

Hasan became very sad when he heard that. "How is it possible for people to have nothing to eat?" he wondered. But then he remembered hearing about those children in the world who are starving every day or only have very little to eat. Hasan remembered, too, that when he did not finish up his supper, his parents would tell him: "You should not waste your food and let it go bad. There are many people in the world who are starving."

"What is more," said Uncle Ismail, "we not only think of the people who have nothing to eat when we fast. We, too, are not eating the whole day long. This means we are eating less, therefore we are saving some food. That food which is saved should be given to the poor who are hungry. Fasting therefore means eating less ourselves in order to give some food to the poor."

"That's a good idea," said Hasan and Laila. "We are going to fast when Ramadan comes. We can tell mother and father to collect the money which is put aside during fasting and then give it to the poor who are hungry. Later, when we are older, we will fast the whole month of Ramadan, then there will be even more money put aside so that the poor can get even more from us."

6. Fasting
(Second Part)

Time passed, and the month of Ramadan arrived. Uncle Ismail had already gone home. Hasan and Laila noticed that their parents woke up earlier than usual, and heard them going to the kitchen. It was still dark and they were eating a meal which they called Sahur.

Hasan and Laila decided to join them. "We want to eat Sahur with you," they said. This was a pleasant surprise for the parents, who were pleased to have such good Muslim children. So, they all sat down and ate together. After that, they performed their early morning prayer together. Then the children went back to sleep.

A while later, Hasan had to get up to go to school. This time there was no breakfast waiting for him, and no sandwich to take to school either. Hasan was hungry, but he did not say anything about it. When noon came, he was hungrier than ever, but he thought of Uncle Ismail who was back in Pakistan. The Muslims in Pakistan would be fasting, too, and Uncle Ismail was surely as hungry as he was. Hasan also thought of what Uncle Ismail had said: the poor are hungry every day. Still, Hasan knew he would get something to eat in the evening and he could also then drink to his heart's content.

As evening approached, Mother laid a small meal on the table. The morning meal is called Sahur, and the evening meal is called Iftar. The family sat down at the table and began to eat. Their hunger was soon gone. Hasan and Laila were very happy that they had gone through their first day of fasting so well.

Later on, they had a real supper. It was delicious and everybody enjoyed it. Shortly after that, the children went to bed. Hasan was very tired, but before falling asleep, his thoughts were again of Uncle Ismail and the reasons he gave for Muslims to fast: they want to be able to share their food with the poor.

Hasan was thankful that he, at least, could eat when evening came. The poor could not do that. They had to be hungry in the evening, too. Hasan then said in his heart: ''I thank Allah for giving me enough to eat.''

He was just about to fall asleep, when he suddenly remembered something. He got out of bed and rushed to his parents. ''Don't forget to wake me up for Sahur,'' he asked them. ''I want to fast again tomorrow, so that the poor will have more to eat.''

After that he crawled back under the blankets and was soon fast asleep.

7. Fasting
(Third Part)

Laila was also awake early next morning. After they had finished Sahur, her mother told her, ''Before fasting, one should also say the Niyya.''

''What is the Niyya?'' asked the children.

''Niyya means intention,'' said Mother. ''When we fast, we say: I am going to fast this day for the whole day, and after saying that, we don't eat any more until evening.''

''How do you say it in Arabic?'' asked Hasan.

''You don't have to say it in Arabic,'' Mother replied, ''but it is quite easy. It is 'Wa bisaumi ghadin nawaitu'.''

''We can say that easily!'' said the children, and they repeated: ''Wa bisaumi ghadin nawaitu.''

That evening, Mother told Hasan and Laila that Muslims must also say a Niyya before starting to eat for Iftar.

She then explained, ''The Niyya means: O Allah, I have fasted this day, and now I shall eat from your nourishment. In Arabic it is: Allahumma laka sumtu wa 'ala rizqika aftartu.''

''Oh dear!'' Hasan remarked, ''That's quite difficult.''

Hasan's father was there and heard what the boy said. ''Yes,'' said Father, ''It is not easy, but if you were to fast every day then you would say it every evening, and you will easily memorize it.''

''All right,'' said Hasan, ''but as I don't know it yet, can you help me with it?''

"Of course I will," Father assured him, "but I think it is best for us to say the Niyya together at the same time. That way, you children can learn it more easily. After that, we can start eating together, too."

After supper, Mother told the children about Lailatu-l-qadr. "Lailatu-l-qadr is one of the nights toward the end of Ramadan," she said. "On this night we stay up late and recite the Qur'an and say many prayers. This is the night when, many years ago, Angel Gabriel spoke for the first time to Prophet Muhammad, telling him to go to the people and bring them Allah's message: Allah has created mankind. Mankind should do good. They should pray to Allah and they should help the poor and the sick."

After hearing that, Hasan understood much better what the angel had said: We Muslims should help the poor, which means we should give them something to eat when they don't have any food. That is why we have the fasting month. Hasan and Laila were already looking forward to the night when they would be able to stay up late for Lailatu-l-qadr.

8. Zakat

When the fasting month of Ramadan came to an end, there was a big celebration. Everybody was happy to have gone through the month of fasting.

Hasan was wondering at the amount of food being served and the many visitors who came to celebrate the occasion. ''Mother must have spent a fortune on groceries,'' he thought. ''I hope she did not spend all the money we have saved to give to the poor.''

That morning, Father had asked Hasan to come to the mosque to pray with him and the other men.

On the way, Hasan asked his father, ''What about the money that we have put aside? Aren't we going to give it to the poor?''

''Of course we are!'' his father assured him. ''In fact, I've already given it to them, for according to Prophet Muhammad, we should do that before going to pray. But that is not all! We are also going to give them some of the delicious food which Mother has cooked. There are poor people here too, and though they are not really starving, they are not doing very well either. So they will be happy to get some of the festive food.''

''How else can one help the poor?'' asked Hasan.

''Well,'' said Father, ''I'll tell you all about it when we get home from the mosque.''

There were many people in the mosque. The men were in front, with the women behind them. Hasan sat next to his father on the floor. After prayer, everybody wished each other 'Id Mubarak', which

means 'Blessed celebration'. The day which comes after the month of Ramadan is called Id-ul-fitr.

On the way back from the mosque, Father said to Hasan, "I was going to tell you about how one can help the poor. According to the Qur'an those who have enough for living, must each year give away to the poor a part of their belongings. In the past, people used to own herds of cattle, camel and sheep or grains, vegetables and fruits. A part of these were given away to the poor. This is what we call Zakat. Nowadays we give Zakat usually in the form of money. If we have 100 pence, the amount we have to give to the poor would be $2\frac{1}{2}$ pence, or $2\frac{1}{2}$ percent."

Hasan was puzzled. "But if we give money to the poor, why are there still so many poor people?" he asked. "If the rich always give to the poor, then surely nobody should be poor."

"I'm afraid it's not as easy as that," said Father. "Unfortunately, not everybody follows this rule of Allah. The rich especially don't follow it because they want to have more and more, so they refuse to give any away."

"I seem to have heard that before," remarked Hasan. "The same thing happened in Makka during Prophet Muhammad's time, didn't it? Why do rich people act so selfishly?"

"Well," said Father, "when a man is rich, he thinks he can buy everything in this world with his money, so he doesn't think of Allah any more. He only thinks of himself and his possessions."

"I don't quite understand that," said Hasan.

"Let me explain it further," Father said. "Now, do you still know how the Shahada begins?"

"Yes," said Hasan, "ashhadu an la ilaha illa llah; this means I bear witness that there is no god apart

from Allah."

"Ah! There is the clue!" Father replied. "You see, Hasan, that is what many people forget when they become rich. They forget that only Allah is great and almighty. They think that because they have a lot of money, they too are great and mighty."

Hasan thought for a while, trying to figure out what his father had said. Then he said: "To give Zakat means to give to the poor so that they will have enough money to live on. On the other hand, this also means that those who give their money to the poor will never get so rich to the point where they start forgetting Allah. Am I right?"

"Yes," said Father, "you certainly are. We pay Zakat every year, and it is not going to bother us that there are many rich people who don't. We obey Allah and we pay Zakat. What the others do is their own business. We are not going to have anything to do with them."

Hasan agreed, and then said, "We fast and pay Zakat to help the poor. But the rich are also our friends on condition that they, too, help the poor. By helping the poor like we do, they are obeying Allah's words, and all those who obey Allah are our friends."

9. Pilgrimage

Three months later, Uncle Ismail came for another visit. This time, he brought Aunt Fatima with him. They had both recently been in Makka for Hajj. Hajj is the Arabic word for pilgrimage.

"There were very many people in Makka. They all came from many different countries," said Uncle Ismail.

"Yes," said Aunt Fatima, "those men and women were in Makka because it is said in the Qur'an that they should go there. As you know, Islam means to say the Shahada, to pray five times a day, to fast in the month of Ramadan, to give Zakat to the poor and to go on the pilgrimage to Makka."

"What did you do there?" asked Laila, very much wanting to know.

"We performed our pilgrimage according to the way Prophet Muhammad taught us," explained Uncle Ismail. "First, we went to a small mountain near Arafat, and stayed there the whole day, praying to Allah. In the evening, we went further till we reached a valley where we collected some small stones. Next day, we came to Mina, which is a small village near Makka. In Mina are three high stone pillars. We threw the pebbles we had collected at the three pillars. As we did that we thought to ourselves: Now we are throwing these stones at Iblis so that he will leave us in peace. When that was over, we slaughtered a sheep."

"I know why you did that," interrupted Hasan. "It

Muslims around the World

was in remembrance of Prophet Ibrahim."

"That's right," said Aunt Fatima. She smiled at Hasan. "My goodness!" she said, "You know a lot already. You can tell me the story of Ibrahim later, alright?"

But there was more to tell about the pilgrimage. Uncle Ismail continued: "Later we went to Makka where the Ka'ba is. The Ka'ba is situated in the centre of the mosque. It is a big stone house with a flat roof and no windows. In fact, it looks like a very big cube. We walked around the Ka'ba and circled it seven times, just as Prophet Muhammad had instructed us."

"Prophet Ibrahim and his son Ismail were the ones who built the Ka'ba," Laila said.

"That's right," said Aunt Fatima. "But do you also know why they did?"

"No," said Laila, "but do tell us!"

"They built the stone house because they were prophets who had heard Allah's words," Uncle Ismail explained. "They obeyed these words, and they wanted other people to be reminded of Allah when they came by the house. That is why Muslims go there for their pilgrimage."

"Can you go inside the house?" asked Laila.

"That's not necessary," replied Uncle Ismail. "It is not really a house, the sort we live in. It's sufficient to see it from the outside. When you circle round the Ka'ba you are reminded that Allah always sent messages to the prophets for mankind. The first of these prophets was Adam and the last was Muhammad. All the prophets said the same thing: You should believe in Allah. He has created you and made plants and animals so that you can live on them. You should pray to Allah and do good."

Uncle Ismail and Aunt Fatima went on talking

127

about Makka and Hasan and Laila listened, fasci
nated. Their Uncle and Aunt had seen so many
different people there. Some of them had very dark
skins, some light, and some very tanned brown. But
despite their difference in appearance, these people
consider themselves brothers and sisters because
they are all Muslims who believe in Allah and follow
what Prophet Muhammad told them.

"When I grow up," thought Hasan to himself, "I
shall go on a pilgrimage to Makka."

10. The Five Pillars of Islam

Islam has five pillars, like a house:

To say the Shahada
To pray five times a day
To fast in the month of Ramadan
To pay Zakat to the needy
To go on a pilgrimage to Makka.

If the pillars are firm, the house will stand firm.
If all Muslims do these five things, Islam will be firm.

1   2   3   4   5

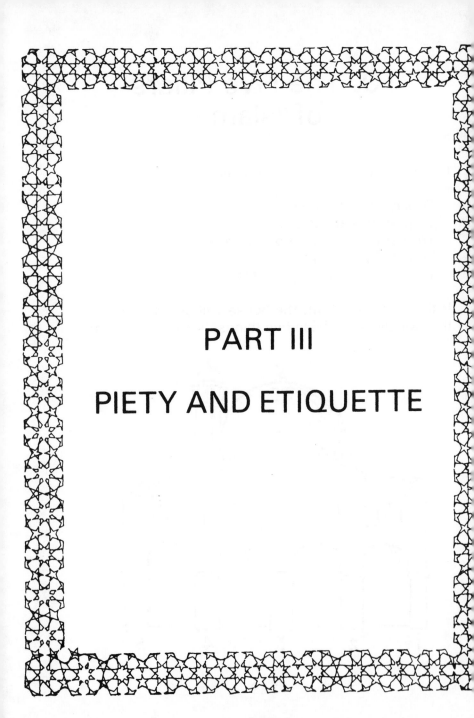

PART III

PIETY AND ETIQUETTE

1. Visitors

Uncle Ismail and Aunt Fatima had come for another visit. This time, they brought their two children with them, their son Ali and their daughter Jamila. They were of the same age as Hasan and Laila.

As they entered the house, they said: "As-salamu alaikum." Hasan and Laila replied: "Wa alaikum salam." They knew that the Prophet had once said that we should always greet others and wish them peace. "As-salamu alaikum" and "wa alaikum salam" means: "Peace be with you" and "with you be peace."

The children played together, even though Hasan and Laila could speak only English and Ali and Jamila did not know any English. In spite of that, they played very well together.

A while later, the children were called for their meal and Laila showed her visitors to the bathroom, where they could wash their hands. After that they went together and sat at the table. Before starting to eat, Ali and Jamila said: "Bismi-llah."

When he heard that, Hasan asked Uncle Ismail, "Why do they say that?"

"It means: 'In the name of Allah'," Uncle Ismail answered. "Before eating, we say: 'In the name of Allah' because the food we have comes from Allah. So we think of Allah before we start to eat. After we have eaten, we say: 'Al-hamdu-li-llah',"

"That means: 'Praise be to Allah'," said Laila.

"That's right," said Aunt Fatima, "we thank Allah

after eating because all we have comes from Allah. But now it's really time to eat!''

Everybody enjoyed the delicious meal. Mother had cooked something extra-special for the visitors. After they had finished eating, Hasan and Laila both said: ''Al-hamdu-li-llah, Praise be to Allah!''

''There is also a Du'a to say after eating,'' said Aunt Fatima. ''It is quite easy: Al-hamdu-li-llahi ladhi at'amana wa saqana wa ja'alna muslimin. That means, Praise be to Allah Who has given us our food and drink and Who has made us Muslims.''

''That's a nice Du'a,'' said Hasan, ''I'm going to learn it right away.'' He then repeated it a few times with the help of Ali and Jamila, and Laila also learned it.

بِسْمِ اللّٰه

اَلْحَمْدُ لِلّٰهِ

اَلْحَمْدُ لِلّٰهِ الَّذِي أَطْعَمَنَا وَسَقَانَا وَجَعَلَنَا مُسْلِمِينَ

2. The Mosque

A mosque is a house in which Muslims pray. Some mosques look like an ordinary house, but most have a tall tower which is called the minaret. When it is time for prayer, the Muadhin, the caller for prayer, goes up the minaret and from there announces the Adhan. Adhan is the call for prayer.

There are quite a few things to see in the mosque. In a big mosque, there are usually wells or several water taps for the Muslims to wash themselves before they go to pray.

Whenever we enter a mosque, we should take off our shoes. There are always carpets or mats laid out on the floor. But nobody should walk on them with their shoes on, because the Muslims pray on them. When we Muslims pray, we touch the floor with our foreheads, so it is very important to keep the floor clean and to allow no-one in wearing shoes.

In the praying hall, there is a niche which is called the Mihrab. The Mihrab shows where the Qibla is. As you already know the Qibla is the direction towards which we pray. This direction points to where the Ka'ba is situated in Makka. The Mihrab is there to show us where to face when praying.

Next to the Mihrab stands a high staircase which is called the Mimbar. This is for the speeches at Friday prayers. The speaker goes up the steps to make his speeches, so that the audience can hear him clearly.

All over the world where Muslims live, they have set up mosques or prayer rooms. When Muhammad

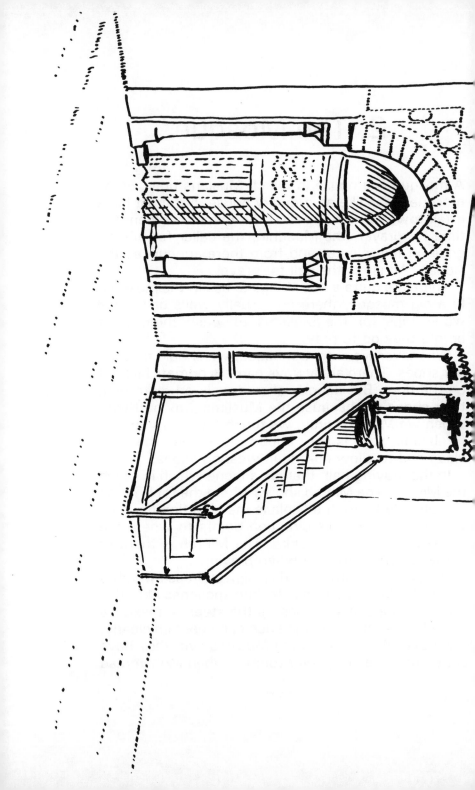

came to Medina, the first thing he did was to build a mosque. The mosque is a place where Muslims pray together to Allah.

الله أكبر الله أكبر
الله أكبر الله أكبر
أشهد أن لا اله الا الله
أشهد أن لا إله إلا الله
أشهد أن محمدا رسول الله
أشهد أن محمدا رسول الله
حي على الصلاة
حي على الصلاة
حي على الفلاح
حي على الفلاح
الله أكبر الله أكبر
لا إله إلا الله

3. Adhan

Before prayer, the Adhan is called.

Allahu akbar   Allahu akbar
Allahu akbar   Allahu akbar
Ashhadu an la ilaha illa-llah
Ashhadu an la ilaha illa-llah
Ashhadu anna Muhammada-rasulu-llah
Ashhadu anna Muhammada-rasulu-llah
Hayya 'ala-salah
Hayya 'ala-salah
Hayya 'ala-l-falah
Hayya 'ala-l-falah
Allahu akbar   Allahu akbar
La ilaha illa-llah

That means:

Allah is great   Allah is great
Allah is great   Allah is great
I bear witness that there is no god apart from Allah
I bear witness that there is no god apart from Allah
I bear witness that Muhammad is Allah's messenger
I bear witness that Muhammad is Allah's messenger
Come to prayer
Come to prayer
Come to Salvation
Come to Salvation
Allah is great   Allah is great
There is no god apart from Allah.

4. Friday Prayer

Every Friday, Father goes to the mosque to pray. The Friday prayer is called Salatul-jum'a. In English it means a congregational prayer because on this day, the Muslims form a gathering or congregation in the mosque.

Before going to the mosque, we should wash ourselves just as we wash for prayer. But it is much better to have a shower before going to Friday prayer. We take off our shoes as soon as we reach the entrance of the mosque. Inside the mosque, we should either go bare foot or only with socks or stockings on.

When Father arrives at the mosque, there are already some people sitting on the floor, reading the Qur'an. The men sit in front and the women at the back.

As more people arrive, and the time for the noon prayer approaches, the Muadhin gives the Adhan, which is the call for prayer. He calls: Allah is great, Muhammad is the Prophet of Allah, and come to prayer. By now, you know what the Adhan sounds like.

The Imam then goes up the Mimbar. An Imam is a Muslim like all the others, but he knows best about the Qur'an. The Mimbar has a number of steps like that of a staircase and the Imam goes up this staircase to make his speech, where everybody can hear him loud and clear. The speech which the Imam makes is called the Khutba. The Imam tells the

people what is written in the Qur'an and says that they should pray only to Allah and always do good.

After the Khutba, the Muadhin calls for the second time. This is called the Iqama. When the people hear it, they know that prayer is about to begin and if they do not hurry, then they will be late.

The Imam then gets down from the Mimbar and stands in front of the Mihrab. The Mihrab is a niche in the wall which shows the direction of Makka. We Muslims always face towards Makka while praying.

The Muslims stand in long rows behind the Imam. Father stands in the row, too. The Imam raises his hands and calls, ''Allahu akbar.'' The people repeat after him. They raise their hands and say, ''Allahu akbar.'' They pray together a prayer with two rak'as, which is as long as the early morning prayer.

The Imam is the man who leads the prayer. The others standing behind him follow exactly what he does. They follow him so that the prayer will not be disorderly. After the prayer is completed, the people say to each other: ''As-salamu alaikum,'' which means Peace be with you. Then, everyone goes home.

5. Tasbih

Whenever Uncle Ismail comes to visit, the children notice that he does not stand up right away after the prayer is ended. Instead, he remains sitting for a little while to say tasbih. Tasbih means to praise Allah. After the prayer, Uncle Ismail says 33 times:

Subhana-llah

That means, Glory be to Allah. Then, he says 33 times:

Alhamdu-li-llah

This means, Praise be to Allah. After he finishes he says 33 times:

Allahu akbar

This means, Allah is great. Uncle Ismail uses his fingers to count. When he is finished, he says a Du'a and after that, he stands up.

سُبْحَانَ اللهِ

الْحَمْدُ لِلّهِ

اللّٰهُ أَكْبَرُ

6. Du'a

Hasan and Laila always say a Du'a after their prayer. Du'a means asking from Allah. Prophet Muhammad taught us many phrases of Du'as which we can use, but we can also make our own Du'as. This is possible even in English.

Prophet Muhammad taught us a Du'a for the morning and for the evening. So every morning when Hasan and Laila wake up, they say: ''Alhamdu-li-Ilahi ladhi ahyana ba'da ma amatana wa ilaihi-nushur.'' This means: ''Praise be to Allah who has woken us up from our deaths and to Allah we shall return.''

Hasan and Laila also know a Du'a for the evening. Before going to sleep, they say: ''Allahumma bismika amutu wa ahya.'' This means: ''O Allah I die and live in Your name.''

اَلْحَمْدُ لِلّٰهِ الَّذِي أَحْيَانَا بَعْدَمَا أَمَاتَنَا وَإِلَيْهِ النُّشُورُ

The Prophet once said that when we are asleep, it is as if we have died, for we are not aware any more of what is happening. That is why Hasan and Laila say the Du'a before sleeping, so that they will sleep well, and wake again the next morning. In the morning when they are awake, they thank Allah because He has woken them up.

In the same way, when we think about it, we can also imagine what life after death is like. Just as we wake up in the morning from our sleep, we will also go on living after we die. We therefore thank Allah for it, and say our Du'as every morning and every evening.

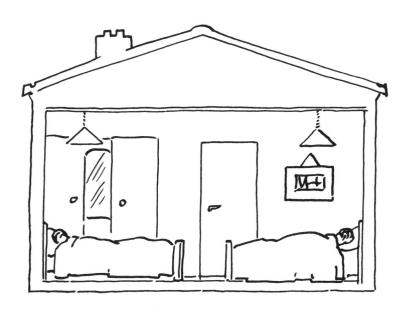

PART IV

CRAFTS AND GAMES

1. The Camel

Camels can be found in many countries where Muslims live. Because camels are very useful animals, they are also very valuable. One should treat all animals well. Camels can carry very heavy loads and can go through many days without water. Whenever they drink, they are able to take in and store a large amount of water.

The Muslims who live in the desert make their clothing and tents out of the camel wool and skin. They also eat the meat of the camel.

Do you still remember what Zakat is? In the past, Muslims paid Zakat with camels. Those who owned more than 25 camels had to give one camel to the poor. Those who owned more than 35 camels had to give a big camel, and those who owned more than 76 camels had to give two camels.

Nowadays, of course, most Muslims don't have that many camels any more, but even so, we still have to give away a part of what we own to the poor. This is what we call Zakat.

You can make yourself a toy camel with some cloth, if you like. All you have to do is to trace out the drawing of the camel twice on a piece of cloth. Cut out and sew the two pieces together with a needle and thread and leave the last bit open. Fill it up with pieces of old cloth or sponge, pushing them in tightly with the end of a pencil. When that is finished, you can sew up the open bit. For the eyes, you can sew on two little buttons or two beads.

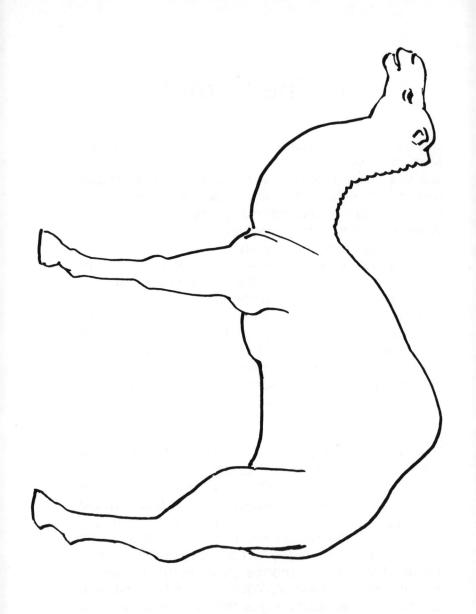

When you play with it, this toy camel can remind you that even today, we should always give part of our belongings to the poor and needy.

JOIN THE DOTS

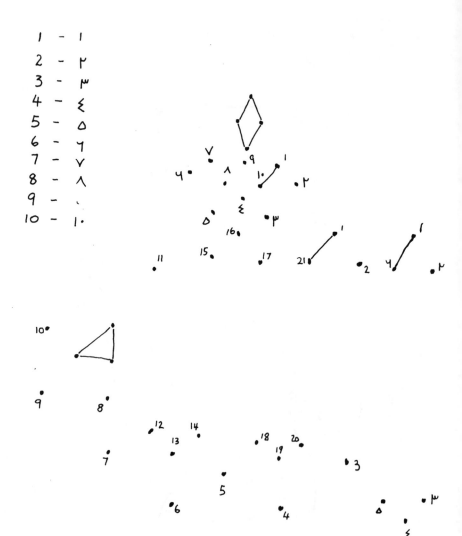

2. Greeting Cards

Do you remember the story of Prophet Ibrahim, who was ordered to kill his son Ismail when Allah wanted to put him to a test? As you know, in remembrance of this occasion, we have a celebration called Id-ul-Adha.

We have also another celebration, which takes place after the end of the month of Ramadan when we have fasted many days. This celebration is called Id-ul-Fitr.

We always look forward to these festive days. Then we give food to the poor or give them other presents, so that they are happy, too. We Muslims share everything with the poor, especially on celebration days.

On these days, Muslims visit each other. However, some friends and relatives live much too far away to visit. So, we send them our greetings to let them know that we are thinking of them. Muslims always have fond feeling for each other especially on these festive occasions.

If you like, you can learn to make your own greeting cards to send to friends or relatives on such festive days. To do this, you will need paper, a pair of scissors, water colour paints or colour pencils and cardboard paper.

An example of a greeting card is given, but you can use your own imagination and make your own design. That should be fun.

Draw your design on the cardboard paper and cut

the picture out. Place the cut-out picture on a piece of paper and colour it. Take care not to use too much water, for the water colours may smear the whole thing. It is best to ask your mother for some old newspapers and put them underneath your painting. After you have finished colouring, take the cardboard paper away very carefully and let the picture dry. In the meantime you can start the next one and, of course, you can make as many cards as you wish.

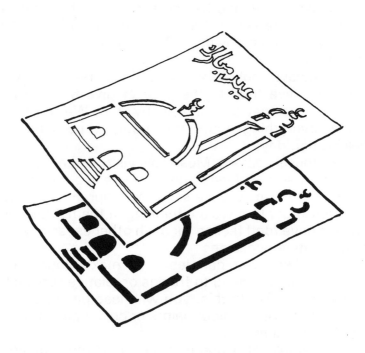

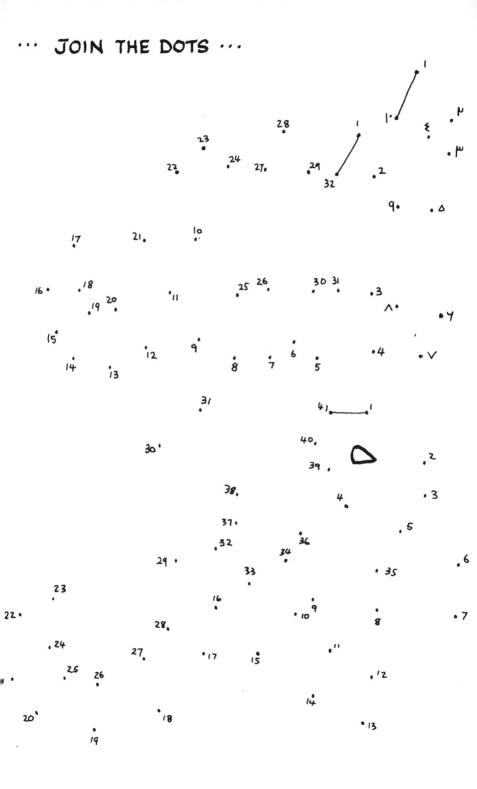

··· JOIN THE DOTS ···

3. The Sundial

The first Muslims who prayed to Allah and followed Prophet Muhammad were very conscientious people. They were also very pious and thought about things which would help them say prayers properly. As you know, they prayed five times a day, so they invented a clock which could tell them when the times for prayer arrived throughout the day.

You, too, can make yourself such a clock, called a sundial. Sundials can still be found in the yards of many old mosques, and they use the rays of the sun to cast a shadow which tells us the time.

Of course, nowadays we have watches and clocks to tell us the times we should pray. However, after you have yourself constructed a sundial, you will realize why pious Muslims were able to make many things. When one is a believer and prays to Allah, one always succeeds in making the most difficult things.

It is not difficult to make a sundial once you know how. The things you will need are: a piece of hard cardboard, a long knitting needle or a long, thin stick, a ruler, a pencil, a pair of scissors and a piece of cork. And of course you will need some gum for sticking.

Cut a rectangle out of the cardboard as big as the given tables, and paste onto both sides of it table A and table B. Place the triangle with the top pointing downwards. Write down the correct times on the lines, as shown in the diagram, and colour it as you wish.

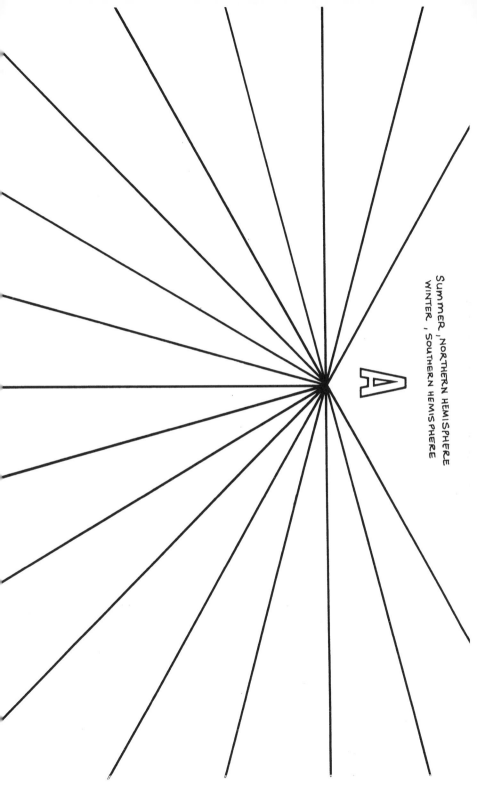

SUMMER, NORTHERN HEMISPHERE
WINTER, SOUTHERN HEMISPHERE

A

WINTER , NORTHERN HEMISPHERE
SUMMER , SOUTHERN HEMISPHERE

B

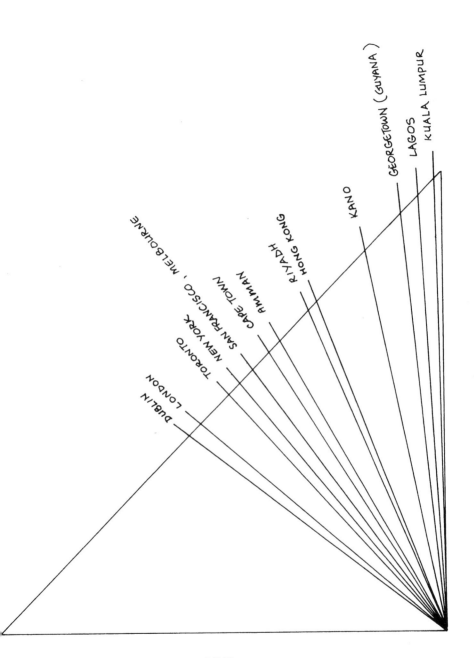

DUBLIN
LONDON
TORONTO
NEW YORK
SAN FRANCISCO, MELBOURNE
CAPE TOWN
AMMAN
RIYADH
HONG KONG
KANO
GEORGETOWN (GUYANA)
LAGOS
KUALA LUMPUR

Make a hole on the spot where all the lines on the table meet and poke the needle or stick through it.

Cut the given diagram of the triangle out of the page along the line which shows the name of the town nearest to you. With the triangle you can determine how big the angle between the needle and the cardboard should be. Look at the diagram to see how the table is placed according to the angle measured from the triangle. After you have the correct position, use the piece of cork to keep the needle firmly in balance. The front side is for summer and the reverse side for winter.

Place the object so that the tip of the needle points towards the North. The shadow which then falls onto the table, with the times numbered on it, shows the correct time.

Now comes a very important question: How can you find out where the North is? Conscientious Muslims also constructed a compass for this purpose, and you too can make one.

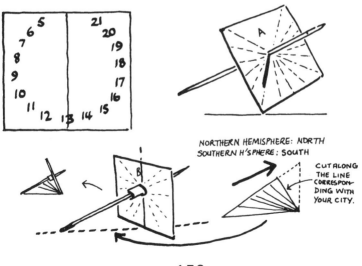

NORTHERN HEMISPHERE: NORTH
SOUTHERN H'SPHERE: SOUTH

CUT ALONG THE LINE CORRESPONDING WITH YOUR CITY.

4. The Compass

A compass is a very practical instrument. You can tell by looking at it where the North is, so that you can place your sundial in the correct position. Besides, with a compass you can also find out where Qibla is, the direction you should face when praying. As you know, we Muslims always face towards Makka where the Ka'ba is when we pray. The religious and conscientious . Muslims made a compass so that they always knew in which direction Makka was.

Should you want to make a compass, the things you would need are: a piece of cork, a long thin needle or a piece of strong wire, some paper and a magnetic pin.

You can make the magnetic pin yourself, even if you do not have a magnet. Borrow a magnet from a friend for a short while. All magnets have two poles. One pole ''pulls'' and the other pole ''pushes''. Take the magnet and a sewing needle or pin and rub the tip a few times with the magnet, starting from the middle of the magnet right up to one end. After that, the pin should be magnetic.

Now, stick the long thin needle or wire onto the piece of cork to make it stand upright. Slide the compass disc with the directions marked on it through the long needle. You can either copy the given diagram of the compass disc or simply cut out the diagram. From the given diagram, you can also see how to mount the magnetic pin onto the needle.

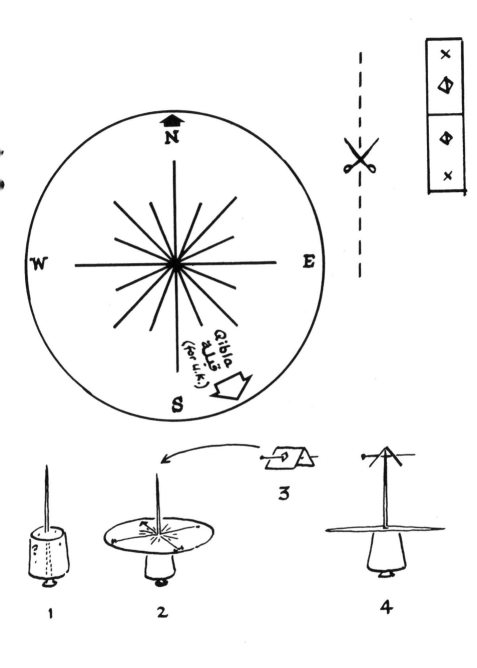

N

W E

Qibla قبلة (for U.K.)

S

1

2

3

4

CROSSWORD NO. 1

Clues

Across:

1. Muslim pilgrimage
3. Quranic Chapter (Arabic)
6. Allah's last Prophet
9. Prophet Jesus
11. He leads the prayer
12. Month for fasting
15. Call to prayer
17. This Prophet built the Kaba, and nearly sacrificed his own son.

Down:

1. Islam's Sacred book (4,5)
2. Friday prayer
3. Islam's first pillar
4. Male sheep
5. Muslim festival
7. The first man and prophet
8. Ibrahim's son
10. Faith (Arabic)
13. Short prayer
14. He built the ark
16. Prophet Muhammad's cousin

CROSSWORD NO. 2

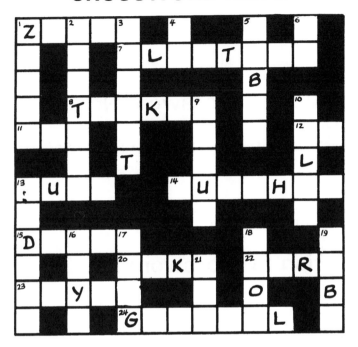

Clues

Across:

1. Due to the poor
7. The first Sura (2,6)
8. The Muslim country was centre of the Ottoman empire
11. Chest bone
12. After Alif
13. Prophet—led his people out of Egypt
14. He calls us to prayer
15. Father of Prophet Sulaiman
20. Unit of prayer
22. Cave where Muhammad was called to prophethood
23. Intention (Arabic)
24. This angel brought the Qur'an to the Prophet

Down:

1. The Book of Prophet Dawud
2. Friday Sermons
3. The Book of Prophet Musa
5. Direction of Makka
6. After Ba
9. Prophet swallowed by a whale
10. He tempts us to disobey Allah
13. City where the Prophet's mosque stands
16. Paths or roads
17. To pull
18. Worn over a Sock
19. Ibrahim built it
21. We cannot breathe without it

Solution to Crossword No. 1

Across:

1:Hajj; 3:Sura; 6:Muhammad; 9:Isa; 11:Imam; 12:Ramadan; 15:Adhan; 17:Ibrahim

Down:

1:Holy Quran; 2:Juma; 3:Shahada; 4:Ram; 5:Id; 7:Adam; 8:Ismail; 10:Iman; 13:Dua; 14:Nuh; 16:Ali

Solution to Crossword No. 2

Across:

1:Zakat; 7:Al Fatiha; 8:Turkey; 11:Rib; 12:Ba; 13:Musa; 14:Muadhin; 15:Dawud; 20:Raka; 22:Hira; 23:Niyya; 24:Gabriel

Down:

1:Zabur; 2:Khutbas; 3:Taurat; 5:Qibla; 6:Ta; 9:Yunus; 10:Iblis; 13:Madina; 16:Ways; 17:Drag; 18:Shoe; 19:Kaba; 21:Air

PASTE THIS PAGE ON A SHEET OF CARDBOARD, CUT OUT THE SHAPES AND TRY TO FIT THEM INTO A PICTURE.

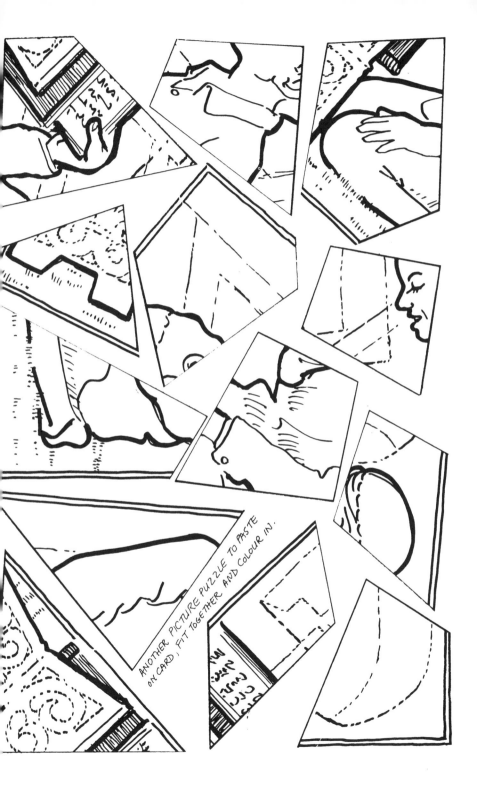

ANOTHER PICTURE PUZZLE TO PASTE ON CARD, FIT TOGETHER AND COLOUR IN.

PART V

A WORD TO PARENTS

A Word to Parents

This book was first written in the German language and published in 1977. There was great demand for it, and the first editions were soon out of print. It will shortly be reprinted once again. The book, both in German and now in English, was meant only as a beginning, not as the complete result of long years of experience and research. It was therefore necessary to set down the precise purpose of its contents:

The problems of Islamic education in non-Islamic surroundings merit very serious consideration. The problem is immense. This became for example evident in 1973, when Dr. Smail Balic (Austria) published a list of 53 Muslim families whose children, bred and reared in a non-Islamic environment, grew up to neglect and ignore their Islamic duties. Dr. Balic was aware of this problem much earlier, and in 1963 had written a study book on Islam for young people and adults, entitled "Call from the Minaret".

More recently, Fatima Heeren in Germany who has helped to give this book its final shape, contributed "The Education of Our Children", a model of Islamic education discussing four phases corresponding to child development stages: Phase 1 — Growing up in an Islamic environment; Phase 2 — Getting to know Islam through tales and stories; Phase 3 — Practising Islam in one's own life by fulfilling religious obligations (the five pillars of Islam); Phase 4 —

Identification with Islam through personal jihad.

The book before you in the main emphasises phases 2 and 3. Dr. Balic's book, (not available in English) as the title itself indicates, is more appropriate for adolescents.

With regard to phase 1, no hard and fast rules can yet be imposed upon a child. An attempt to cover phase 2 has been made by the Islamic Centre in Hamburg with the publication of "A Book of Religion for Muslim Children", which was of some assistance in preparing the present book. In addition, we also have in this book a combination of phases 2 and 3. To this end, we have made "Learning about Islam" and "Practising Islam" as compact as possible.

The book now before you is for parents and for their children. Parents should not feel that by giving their child this book they are relieved of their responsibilities. On the contrary, the actual purpose is to get parents and children to work together. It is very necessary that parents themselves personally take part in conveying the contents of this book to their children. The attentive adult who goes through the book will soon discover that in most stories told here only the basic framework is set. This leaves ample opportunity for parents and teachers to include more material from the Qur'an that relates to the particular stories.

It is of prime importance to make our children familiar with Islam from a very early age and to give them a proper Islamic education. Otherwise, environmental influences will distract and alienate them from Islam. As in most cases children get little chance to attend regular religious classes, this book may be used as a help to fill this gap. It can be used within the family itself, in small groups or whenever possible, in religious lessons in the classroom. Since we are forced to do without Islamic education in schools, we have to replace it for the time being with a suitable alternative, until one day, hopefully, we will solve this problem more satisfactorily.

As English is the language spoken in England and in many other parts of the world, we have rendered this book into English. In this way, we aim at taking Islam out of an isolation rooted in the multilingualism of our children. Usually, when Islam is taught this is done in the mother tongue. However, a substantial number of Muslim children are actively involved in speaking English and many of them even outside this country attend English medium schools. By teaching our children Islam in English we can help them accept Islam in their own personal lives and so accentuate its importance to them.

Multilingualism can be a barrier. Should we fail to overcome it, then this will be a very serious failure. For in that case, the first step has been taken in alienating our children from Islam and the Islamic world. In that case, the validity of Islam for our children would be limited to certain occasions, and perhaps not even those. As adults, we must unfortunately accept that our life as Muslims is no longer ideal, and that makes it all the more important that we do as much as we can for our children.

To bring up our children to be religious, we need to define what religion means, and in our case Islam. Islam is our way of life, which we live in accordance with the principle of tawhid, the oneness of God. The confession of absolute monotheism is the outstanding characteristic of a Muslim. It frees him of anything that does not appertain to the one and only God.

This is also the basic foundation of our book. The things we want to draw attention to are: (1) the unrelenting fact of tawhid; (2) the effects on individual lives through confessing tawhid; (3) the effect on the community. Our way of life consists of three things: we live with the confession of tawhid as an individual and in a community. By this we don't mean the ideal Islamic society to which we hope to aspire, but are limiting it for the moment to our present circumstances; living in Europe within a non-Islamic society.

Furthermore, to provide a child with Islamic education in a non-Islamic society demands two things: a child must be able to acquire Islamic information from his own surroundings. In our special case, great care must be taken that he first experiences at home what Islam means. We can neither expect him to gather this information outside the home nor in school as he grows up. Secondly, it is obvious that he will be confronted with the fact that he is different from other, non-Muslim children. We must be conscious of the fact that an Islamic education does not make things easier for a child living in non-Islamic surroundings. It is therefore our responsibility to pay extra attention to his well-being and healthy progress in spiritual matters.

According to Abu Hurairah's report, the Prophet once said: ''All children are born Muslims, it is only the parents who make Jews, Christians and Magians out of them.'' (Bukhari and Muslim).

Today this statement has significance in a very specific way: it does not depend entirely on us and our education whether a child becomes a Jew, Christian or Magian. But our important task is to live and practise Islam, so that our child has the opportunity to grow up as a Muslim. It is not sufficient to have our children learn Islam at home, in the mosque or even in school without the parents themselves taking it seriously. For then, the Islamic education would turn out to be a mere formality, and would be left behind as the children grow up. That is why this book is both for parents and children: on one's own, one either cannot be a Muslim or becomes a Muslim under great difficulty.

This book consists of four parts apart from "A Word to Parents". Part I introduces in the form of tales what is traditionally understood as "Iman". It deals with the fundamental beliefs, namely: Allah, angels, prophets, books of revelation, resurrection and good and evil. Special stress is of course given to stories of the prophets. The "leitmotiv" recurring in the stories emphasizes the fact that all prophets told man: "Pray to Allah — Allah has created you — He made plants and animals for you to eat — Man should be grateful and do good". These four dominant topics should be brought into discussions with the child.

As explained in the story of Adam, prophets were persons who brought to mankind God's revelation displayed in the "leitmotiv": "We pray to Allah — He is our creator and sustainer — we do good." Try to make the child acquainted with these stories as bedtime stories and by asking them questions on already known prophets. The child should understand that all the prophets had one common task and were sent by one single god, Allah.

Encourage the child to colour the simple illustrations in the book. Do take time to make the child repeat to you the respective stories depicted by the illustrations when he proudly shows to you one he has just coloured. The child will enjoy it more if you show your appreciation, and at the same time, you are also controlling his learning process. Such responses would increase the child's interest in the stories.

The general approach is to interest and occupy the child as fully as possible according to his capabilities and age. The fourth part is especially intended to motivate children of all ages with instructions for skill craft and games.

The five pillars of Islam are introduced in the second part of the book. The prayer is stressed here. Some steps towards learning it have been previously introduced in the story section, which includes short paragraphs of prayer words and Surahs. The parents are here asked once more to pay extra attention to the child and especially to give him a good example to follow.

Next to prayer, the importance of Zakat is also mentioned. The story dealing with it aims to connect an early sense of community-spirit, the confession of Islam and wealth and poverty, the contradictions of which do not yet reach a child's understanding or knowledge. In connection with this it should be established in the child's conscience that Islam means active solidarity with the poor in this world and that wealth has no value in itself unless it is used in accordance with Islamic morality.

The less extensive third part is an attempt to put forward the basic foundation in building up a pious personality. The suggestions given are not to be considered complete. As already mentioned, this book does not aim at achieving perfection. We are more concerned that our children believe in and begin to act according to the teachings of Islam; in other words, to prepare them for the start of a long journey.

This book is so composed that it can be of use in religious classes and community centres as well as within the family. The way it is used outside must be similar to that within a family. The subjects for learning and story-telling are to be combined with colouring and craftwork as this makes learning more enjoyable.

Users of this book are requested to inform the author of criticisms and suggestions they may have. This book is, as you know, only a beginning. Therefore your experiences, wishes and opinions will greatly help in preparing future books for our children. The Islamic education of our children is much too urgent a matter to neglect, so we ask you to co-operate with us.

"O you who believe! If you help Allah's cause, He will help you and make your foothold firm." (Surah Muhammad, verse 7.)